The Nazi economic recovery 1932–1938

Second edition

New Studies in Economic and Social History

Edited for the Economic History Society by
Michael Sanderson
University of East Anglia, Norwich

This series, specially commissioned by the Economic History Society, provides a guide to the current interpretations of the key themes of economic and social history in which advances have recently been made or in which there has been significant debate.

In recent times economic and social history has been one of the most flourishing areas of historical study. This has mirrored the increasing relevance of the economic and social sciences both in a student's choice of career and in forming a society at large more aware of the importance of these issues in their everyday lives. Moreover specialist interests in business, agricultural and welfare history, for example, have themselves burgeoned and there has been an increased interest in the economic development of the wider world. Stimulating as these scholarly developments have been for the specialist, the rapid advance of the subject and the quantity of new publications make it difficult for the reader to gain an overview of particular topics, let alone the whole field.

New Studies in Economic and Social History is intended for students and their teachers. It is designed to introduce them to fresh topics and to enable them to keep abreast of recent writing and debates. All the books in the series are written by a recognised authority in the subject, and the arguments and issues are set out in a critical but unpartisan fashion. The aim of the series is to survey the current state of scholarship, rather than to provide a set of prepackaged conclusions.

The series has been edited since its inception in 1968 by Professors M. W. Flinn, T. C. Smout and L. A. Clarkson, and is currently edited by Dr Michael Sanderson. From 1968 it was published by Macmillan as *Studies in Economic History*, and after 1974 as *Studies in Economic and Social History*. From 1995 *New Studies in Economic and Social History* is being published on behalf of the Economic History Society by Cambridge University Press. This new series includes some of the titles previously published by Macmillan as well as new titles, and reflects the ongoing development throughout the world of this rich seam of history.

For a full list of titles in print, please see the end of the book.

The Nazi economic recovery 1932–1938

Second edition

Prepared for the Economic History Society by

R. J. Overy
King's College, London

CAMBRIDGE
UNIVERSITY PRESS

Published by the Press Syndicate of the University of Cambridge
The Pitt Building, Trumpington Street, Cambridge CB2 1RP
40 West 20th Street, New York, NY 10011-4211, USA
10 Stamford Road, Oakleigh, Melbourne 3166, Australia

The Nazi Economic Recovery 1932–1938 first published by The Macmillan
Press Limited 1982
Reprinted 1984, 1989, 1990 (twice), 1991, 1993, 1994
Second edition first published by Cambridge University Press 1996

Printed in Great Britain at the University Press, Cambridge

A catalogue record for this book is available from the British Library

A catalogue record for this book is available from the Library of Congress

ISBN 0 521 55286 9 hardback
ISBN 0 521 55767 4 paperback

CE

Contents

Acknowledgements

I am grateful to the following for their helpful advice and encouragement in the preparation of the first edition of this book: Professors Donald Coleman, Harold James, Alice Teichova and Norman Stone. I would like to thank Professor Smout for his sound editorial guidance. For the second edition there is only myself to blame. The new version owes a great deal to a wealth of literature on the Nazi economy that has appeared in German over the last decade and a half. It is not possible to give adequate recognition in a book like this to all the individual authors whose work has helped to re-shape the new edition, and I hope a collective acknowledgement can express the debt I owe.

Note on references

References in the text within square brackets relate to the numbered items in the Bibliography, followed, where necessary, by the page numbers in italics, for example [1: *1–10*].

1
Introduction: some perspectives

The story of the German economy between 1929 and 1938 is a critical one in the history of modern Germany. Historians and economists still debate the issues of the depression in the hope of showing that different economic policies might have stopped Hitler. The economic recovery that followed raised then, and since, important questions about the relationship between state and economy, questions that have come more clearly into focus with renewed emphasis in recent years on markets rather than state initiative in the developed economies. More controversially, the economic recovery stands at the centre of any 'positive' view of the Third Reich. If there is still disagreement about how the Nazi economy should be interpreted, there is a general consensus that recovery did occur at a faster rate and to a higher level than almost anywhere else in Europe. Since a central feature of the revival was the regime's willingness to undertake schemes of deficit financing, the myth has taken root that Hitler was a Keynesian before Keynes, and being so won widespread support inside Germany in the years of peace and returning prosperity.

While there is some truth in this picture, it is in general misleading. The economic recovery must be placed in a wider perspective. Indeed the very term 'recovery' is in some sense ambiguous. The German economy was relatively stagnant in the inter-war years. Two short bursts of high growth (1925–8 and 1937–9) punctuated a general picture of slow growth, economic discontent and painful adjustment to the changed and unhealthy climate of the inter-war world economy. There is no disputing the fact that the German economy recovered from the disastrous trough reached in business activity in 1932. But throughout the

Table I *Annual average growth rates in Germany of selected economic indices 1870/1913–1950/70*

	1870–1913	1913–50	1913–38	1950–60	1950–70
Growth of total production	2.9	1.2	2.6	7.6	6.2
Growth of output per capita	1.8	0.4	–	6.5	5.3
Growth of output per man-hour	2.1	0.9	1.3	6.0	5.0
Growth of exports (volume)	11.0	−2.4	−1.6	16.0	12.8
Fixed investment as % of GNP (excl. housing)	15.6*	–	9.7*	16.1	17.7

* Figures for 1900–13 and 1920–38.

inter-war years the German economy failed on average to match the growth rates of pre-1914 or the high rates achieved after 1950. Trade revived slowly in the 1920s and collapsed in the 1930s. Domestic consumer demand responded sluggishly in both decades. Productivity improved significantly only with the so-called 'rationalisation' movement in the mid-1920s, and then for a limited range of industrial sectors. Full employment later in the 1930s paid the price of a slower and more uneven growth of productivity. Wages barely recovered to the level of 1913 in real terms. It was the exceptional decline of the depression years from 1929 to 1932 which gave the subsequent revival its rosy complexion. Table I sets out the long-term growth record. Average annual performance compared poorly with other industrial states, even with Mussolini's Italy. International comparisons are set out in Table II. The German economic miracle was very much a product of the post-Nazi era, not of the 1930s.

The recovery must also be contextualised in other ways. It is sometimes suggested that the recovery was a product of a specific 'fascist' economic strategy, which distinguished it from the recovery

Table II *Comparative economic performance of selected countries 1913–1937/8 (1913 = 100)*

	GNP (1937)	Ind. output (1937–8)	Output per man-hour (1938)	Real wages	Annual rate of growth*
USA	171.9	164	208	153	2.9%
Sweden	174.0	231	143	150	2.2%
Italy	154.2	196	165	n.a.	1.3%
UK	146.5	139	167	133	1.7%
Germany	136.4	144	137	109	1.2%
France	120.8	119	178	128	0.7%

* 1913–50.

efforts of other capitalist states. While few would disagree that the Nazi regime had a number of clear ideological preferences when it came to the economy (or that these came to determine the direction that the economy was to take by the late 1930s) the policies actually pursued in 1933 had much in common with those adopted in other countries, and with the policies of the pre-Hitler governments. The control of foreign exchange movements, work-creation and intervention in the formation of prices and wages were all in fact the products of the pre-Hitler period, modified or extended by the new regime after 1933. The German economy traditionally enjoyed a higher degree of state regulation or inter-vention than the more liberal western economies. Under the impact of war, defeat, hyperinflation in 1923 and the crash in 1929, state involvement became more widespread and increasingly necessary. In the 1920s state spending was double the pre-war levels.

A higher level of state economic intervention cannot be regarded as intrinsically fascist, and indeed German strategy for combating the slump has been compared with the anti-depression policies pursued in Roosevelt's New Deal [36; 107]. State deficit-finan-cing, the regulation of trade and currency transactions, state stimulation of heavy industry and construction, and the super-vision of banking and capital markets could all be found in one mix or another in the anti-depression armoury of the rest of the world. They were the product of circumstantial pressures as much as ideology – the decline of world trade, the collapse of world prices, high unemployment, and the unwillingness of private investors to plough their money into the productive sectors.

Why then should the German recovery have occasioned so much debate? Part of the answer is economic. The German experience in the inter-war years was an extreme manifestation of the business cycle in operation. Explanation for both the severity of the collapse and the speed of the revival offered lessons to modern economists wrestling since the 1970s with a slower and more uneven pattern of growth in the developed world. Another answer lies in the apparently demonstrable links between economic performance and radical politics in inter-war Germany. The depression was inextricably bound to the course of German party politics; economic policy choices were shaped by political expectations as much as by economic circumstance. The rise of Nazism as an electoral force is widely regarded as a direct consequence of the failure of government economic strategy during the slump. The consolidation of the Nazi dictatorship between 1933 and 1936 was eased by the subsequent business revival, which secured for Hitler a broader base of approval than he had enjoyed in 1932 [87]. To understand the business cycle, so the argument goes, is to understand the political cycle too.

There are, finally, profound disagreements about how to interpret both the causes and course of the recession, and how to explain the recovery that followed. In what follows, the international and political contexts feature where appropriate, but the main focus is on the economic explanation for the fall and rise of the German economy in the 1930s.

2
The German economy from war to depression

On the eve of the First World War Germany possessed all the features of an advanced and expanding industrial economy. German trade was on the point of exceeding that of Great Britain. Output had increased at the rate of almost 3 per cent a year for forty years. German industry was highly competitive and was supported by a banking system and educational structure particularly favourable to industrial growth. Economic modernisation was reflected, too, in the changing social structure. Bismarck's Germany in 1871 had been predominantly rural; Germany in 1913 was predominantly, though by no means completely, industrial. The Great War did not reverse the direction taken by the German economy in any permanent way, but it did seriously distort the trajectory of economic development. A combination of territorial losses, particularly the industrial regions of Alsace-Lorraine, Silesia and the Saarland, together with the collapse of German trade and the shortage of capital, contributed to a decline in industrial output in the years 1919–24 to between half and three-quarters of the level of 1913. The costs of war and reconstruction also fuelled a high rate of inflation, which led to the collapse of the German mark in 1923 and the loss of half a century of accumulated savings.

In the years following inflation the economy struggled to regain the achievements of 1913. The revival of industrial output, though it lagged behind that of the rest of Europe and far behind that of the United States, did lead by 1928 to a restoration of the output and trade levels of the pre-war period. The revival rested heavily on foreign investment which provided the resources that the domestic capital market lacked following the inflation. Foreign funds made possible a limited modernisation programme for sections of German industry. Between 1925 and 1929, output per man-hour in the major industrial sectors expanded by 17 per cent; large industrial plant was built, to exploit modern production methods. Technological innovation, which had been slowed down by the impact of war, once again became an important component in the growth of Germany's industrial core [33; 50].

The recovery in the 1920s disguised many structural weaknesses. It was a fragile revival, restoring pre-war achievements but exhibiting few signs of sustained expansion and buoyant growth as in the years before 1914. Looked at in the long-term, it is difficult to dispute Petzina's conclusion that the 1920s, or for that matter much of the inter-war period as a whole, was for Germany a period of relative economic stagnation. Whereas GNP doubled in Germany between 1890 and 1913, and trebled between 1950 and 1970, it increased by only 4 per cent between 1913 and 1929 [75: *10–74*]. The causes of sluggish development were many. The terms of the peace settlement in 1919 were designed to hold back German economic revival: the territories lost to Poland and France contained three-quarters of Germany's iron ore, and one-third of her coal; 90 per cent of the German merchant fleet was confiscated; all Germany's overseas assets, totalling 16 billion marks, were forfeited. Above all the victors insisted that Germany pay for their war losses, and imposed a final bill for reparations of 132 billion gold marks.

Germany entered the world market again after the war already disadvantaged. But the slow revival of world trade, and the worsening terms of trade for primary producing countries in particular, hit the German economy harder than most because of its high export dependence. Before the war, exports supplied 22 per cent of the national product; in 1928 the figure was only 16 per cent. In the German boom of the 1950s and 1960s the export quota reached 25 per cent [59: *15*]. Germany's share of world exports fell 31 per cent between 1913 and 1927–9, even further than Britain's. Germany's trade with primary producers fell by more than a third over the same timescale. The decline in European capital export in the 1920s also hit German trade, because it reduced demand for German goods in markets financed before the war by British and French credits. The poor trade performance exaggerated the reparations problem, which constituted an additional burden on the German balance-of-payments. If it can be argued that Germans exaggerated the economic burden of reparations in the 1920s for political reasons, it cannot be ignored altogether. War debts were a constant source of friction between Germany and the victor states, who had expected reparations to be paid out of a growing German trade surplus. In fact Germany ran a trade deficit for most of the 1920s; reparations ended up being paid, in effect, by foreign investors attracted to Germany's high interest rates [92]. The reliance on foreign credit tied Germany into a dangerous dependency on the world's financial markets at a time when there existed serious structural weaknesses in the world monetary and payments system [25].

Germany's troubled relationship with the world economy was compounded with significant domestic constraints on growth, producing what Borchardt has called 'the crisis before the crisis' [59]. A basic problem lay with the German capital market. After the inflation, German interest rates remained at what were then perceived to be exceptionally high levels. The high cost of money reflected a shortage of savings following the inflation, and an understandable reluctance to run risks on the part of German investors. Although capital shortages were made good to some extent by large imports of money from abroad, the investment ratio in the 1920s remained well below the pre-war level, while smaller industrial producers, artisans and peasant farmers were left short of capital or were forced to pay for funds at usurious rates. Since craftsmen and peasants made up well over one-third of the working population, the problems they faced acted as a serious drag on the overall performance of the economy.

The sustained industrial and trade growth of the pre-war years had disguised the survival of large numbers of smaller and more marginal producers. The unhappier economic climate of the 1920s exposed the social and structural imbalance of the German economy. German agriculture was unable to compete with more efficient farmers in Europe or against cheap overseas imports. Much of it was small in scale – more than three million holdings – and relatively unmodernised. The long-term decline in agricultural prices in the 1920s, coupled as it was to growing farm indebtedness – an increase from 4.6 billion marks in 1924 to 11.5 billion in 1929 – and to higher taxes and social payments, reduced agricultural incomes and the demand for goods from rural areas. The deterioration of terms of trade for Germany's own primary producers meant that they could afford to buy fewer manufactured goods than before the war. While manufactures increased in price by 57 per cent between 1913 and 1929, farm products increased by only 30 per cent [75: *107*]. There were few gains in agricultural productivity. Mechanisation was held up through the shortage of funds, and farm labour stayed put. The farming population, which had declined more or less continuously as a proportion of the employed population between 1850 and 1913, remained at roughly the pre-war level until 1933. The slow revival of domestic demand during the 1920s owed a good deal to the survival of a numerous, but relatively poor, rural community [75: *104–6*].

Things were not much better among the small shopkeepers and craftsmen. Since they too constituted a sizeable proportion of the German population, some 13 per cent in the 1925 census of occupations, and since they were, like the peasantry, suffering a relative decline throughout the 1920s as they competed with cheaper foreign products and the switch to factory production at home, it is fair to assume that artisan hardships also served to depress domestic demand. Some craftsmen, it is true, found work as skilled factory hands, but many were located away from the main areas of large-scale industry. Nor was the labour market favourable to the displaced craft worker. The modernisation of large-scale industry brought increases in output and productivity, but it left a million workers unemployed [23: *265*; 59: *16*]. The result was low job mobility from countryside to town, or between regions, leading, as Bessel has shown for East Prussia, to significant differences in economic performance both within and between the major provinces [11].

Public spending provided some cushion against the slow growth of demand and rising unemployment. In 1928 public authorities were responsible for 47 per cent of all building work in Germany. Road-building, electrification and the development of municipal services all helped to maintain business activity and stimulate demand as they were later to do under the Nazi regime, but they did so at the price of drawing in large foreign loans during the 1925–9 period that left the German economy very vulnerable to shifts in the world economy [28: *54*; 86: *197*].

If there were losers in German society in the 1920s, there were also winners. Because the economic cake had shrunk in post-war Germany, there developed a conflict over how it should be distributed. Creditors lost their slice when the inflation wiped out savings; peasants and artisans remained marginal to the conflict. The chief beneficiaries of the distributional fight were wage earners, particularly the unionised factory workforce. It is now widely argued that the Weimar system was loaded in favour of labour, whose revolutionary potential had to be bought off with high wage settlements and welfare, which were paid for by taxing industry and farmers more heavily. Wage settlements between unions and employers were fixed in the late 1920s at real levels well above the gains in productivity, with the result that profits, and hence investment, were squeezed – not unlike the situation in Britain in the 1970s.

It is certainly the case that the 'wage ratio' – wages as a proportion of national income – was exceptionally high in the second half of the 1920s. The ratio was 70 per cent in 1910–13, but 87 per cent in 1925–9 (in the 1930s it was to fall to 59 per cent). The statistical evidence on real wages and output, though subject to significant margins of error, does suggest that real-wage growth exceeded productivity gains by a growing margin [59: *139–42*]. Von Kruedener has demonstrated that social spending and taxes both rose faster than output. In this sense the Weimar welfare state was more than a low growth economy could afford. The redistribution of the cake to workers and the state had, it is argued, the effect of squeezing profits and investment funds, and reducing the competitiveness of German exports. German workers, it appears, wanted to have their capitalist cake and eat it at the same time [13; 51].

There are a number of objections that might be made to this argument. The exceptionally high wage ratio is characteristic of a stagnating economy with low investment rates, but is not necessarily the cause of that imbalance. The ratio also disguises the timing and distribution of wage increases. For most workers in the 1920s, wages were below the real levels achieved by 1913, often significantly below. Only in the last two years of the decade was the real wage position recovered, and then not for every region or occupation. Workers did not achieve a significantly higher standard of living, but after ten years of war and inflation they wanted to return to the position they had lost. Balderston has suggested that the high wage settlements of 1927–8 actually reflected local labour scarcity rather than union muscle, a product of rigidities in the labour market [7: *401–2*].

It can also be argued that the low level of productive investment was as much a product of high interest rates, excess capacity and poor expectations of the market as it was of high unit labour costs. The same holds for export competitiveness. Balderston has again shown that German exports were not particularly price sensitive – many were high-value, custom-built products – but were depressed by the poor state of overseas markets or were victims of tariff discrimination. He sees high wages as an effect of export growth rather than a cause of export decline. Holtfrerich has taken the argument about confusing cause and effect one step further: the problem of the German economy in the late 1920s can be seen not as one of high wages, but as one of managerial conservatism and entrepreneurial caution. During the 1920s German industry became highly cartelised, protecting the weaker and less efficient producers, keeping prices artificially high and reaching domestic and international market agreements to limit competition. Its response to a hostile market was to limit damage by collective defence – 'organised capitalism' as it was known – rather than run higher risks and squeeze out the marginal producer [59: *76–8*].

Shifting the blame from workers to entrepreneurs begs other questions about where the investment funds were to be found in order to achieve a more vigorous, modernising capitalism, or where the extra demand for German goods might be generated. It also produces an unnecessary polarity between the two explanations, for they can be seen as complementary rather than as alternatives. Both labour and business in the 1920s were anxious to protect their interests in an uncertain economic climate. They both acted defensively – unions in order to protect nominal wage rates, industry in order to keep up prices and protect market shares. The result was a stalemate: the unions were reluctant to accept the wage restraint which might have generated higher profits and investment and the prospect of future wage increases; business was reluctant to run the risks of more aggressive market capitalism which might have put it, as it did in the 1950s, in the position to pay higher wages and welfare. This was a psychological problem as well as an economic one. With different expectations the stalemate might have been broken.

The sluggish performance of the economy in the 1920s was the result of a number of interdependent causes. There may not even have been a primary cause. Much the same could be said of the German slump that followed between 1929 and 1932, though it has not stopped historians from searching for one. Of course the fragile state of the economy in the 1920s, the 'crisis before the crisis', explains why the slump was so severe and lasted so long, but it does not on its own explain the onset or course of the crisis. There are two approaches to the immediate origins of the German slump. The conventional view was to see it as a direct consequence of the collapse of the American stock market in October 1929 – the Wall Street Crash – and the withdrawal of foreign credits from Germany which followed. The other approach sees the slump as largely a product of domestic forces, exacerbated, but not caused, by the American crash.

In any discussion of the depression the question of foreign lending is clearly crucial. Germany borrowed large sums of money during the 1920s, the bulk of it from the United States. Money was loaned, both long-term and short-term, but tended to be reloaned within Germany on a long-term basis, making it difficult to repay short-term lending should it suddenly be recalled. The extent of such borrowing and capital flows into and out of Germany is set out in Table III. Up to 1928 the bulk of foreign lending was long-term. In 1927 however there was a switch to more short-term lending, and it is to fluctuations in this short-term lending that the downswing of the German economy has generally been attributed. Falkus has maintained that the German economy depended on foreign lending to maintain a satisfactory level of domestic credit, and that since so much of the lending passed through the German banks any reduction in capital supplies from abroad would have the effect of producing a credit squeeze, higher interest rates and a fall-off in business activity [30: 462–5]. The evidence seems to suggest that foreign lending played just such a role. From the middle of 1928 onwards both short- and long-term lending slowed down, interest rates rose, imports of raw materials declined, industrial investment and employment levels began to fall. During

Table III *German balance of payments 1927–32 (m. RM)*

	1927	1928	1929	1930	1931	1932
Current a/c balance	−4244	−931	−2469	−601	1040	257
Net long-term lending	1703	1788	660	967	126	−36
Net short-term lending	1779	1335	765	117	477	−763
Other capital movements	310	1000	879	−594	−3496	286
Capital a/c balance	3792	4123	2304	490	−2693	−513

Source: C. R. Harris, *Germany's Foreign Indebtedness* (1935) pp. 112, 114.

1929 the situation became worse, with net capital imports falling from 4.3 billion marks in 1928, to only 2.7 billion in 1929. The outflow of funds was caused partly by the greater attraction of American sources of investment, and partly by German investors trying to find a safer home abroad for their capital because of the signs that the German economy was entering a period of slow or declining growth and was a less secure, and less profitable, proposition than in 1927 and 1928.

It is over this very question that the role of foreign lending becomes far less clear-cut. If Germany was a less attractive investment prospect in 1928 it is easy to see why. The structural problems already discussed – the slow revival of consumer demand, the crisis in agriculture, the slow expansion of trade and the problem of reparations – all contributed to the fragility of the German recovery. The price of German industrial shares declined from a peak reached as early as April 1927. Industrial investment began to turn down in 1928, inventory investment fell by 1.7 billion marks in the same year, unemployment began to rise from mid-1928 and had already reached 2.8 million by March 1929. It is tempting to see this slow march into depression (so different from the dramatic and sudden collapse in the United States) as Temin and Borchardt have seen it, as the result of a demand crisis in Germany that discouraged businessmen from a continued course of expansion in 1928 [13; 106: *246–8*]. There is certainly evidence that demand was slackening off well before the reduction in levels of foreign lending. The output of consumer goods of elastic demand, the durables that were sustaining other economies, turned downwards as early as February 1928. Net agricultural income was lower in 1928 than 1927. Moreover a close examination of the loans floated in 1928 and 1929 shows that the bulk were directed towards local government in Germany or towards utility investment and that the demand for loans by major German businesses had already slackened off well before the absolute decline in foreign loans.

It is difficult not to conclude under these circumstances that the depression in Germany was a result of both endogenous and exogenous factors, a fall in foreign lending and a deterioration of the balance of payments coinciding with a sharp slowing down of the expansion of the economy due to structural constraints on demand growth. The balance of evidence suggests that the relative stagnation of the German economy in the 1920s, the rise in costs and the slow revival of demand at home and abroad produced a downswing in the economy some time before the decline in foreign lending became significant.

Once the depression had begun to bite in 1929, however, there was no question but that it was made very much worse by the peculiar relationship that Germany had established with the world capital market in the years 1925–9. In 1929, both before and after the Great Crash, funds flowed rapidly out of Germany, but were more than made up for by funds flowing in. In 1930 there was a very small balance in Germany's favour. In 1931 a large-scale net outflow of domestic and foreign funds produced a massive liquidity crisis at both a national and an international level. What might have been a 'normal' business-cycle downswing turned into an economic catastrophe because of the recall of short-term loans and the drying up of long-term lending [34: 55–8]. Against such a background some of the more positive aspects of the depression such as the active balance of trade (achieved for the first time in 1931) and the rapid increase in real incomes for those in employment were of little consolation.

The depression between 1929 and 1932 was characterised by a sharp fall in prices, particularly agricultural prices, very high levels of unemployment and business failure, a sharp and sustained fall in investment activity of all kinds and a fall in government

Table IV *The depression in Germany 1928–32*

	1928	1929	1930	1931	1932
GNP (bn RM)	89.5	89.7	83.9	70.4	57.6
National income (bn RM)	75.4	76.0	70.2	57.5	45.2
Industrial production (1928 = 100)	100.0	100.1	87.0	70.1	58.0
Exports (bn RM)	12.3	13.5	12.0	9.6	5.7
Imports (bn RM)	14.0	13.5	10.4	6.7	4.7
Unemployment (m.)	1.4	1.8	3.1	4.5	5.6

Source: [42: *31*].

spending faster than that of national income. There was a large-scale collapse of industrial output and levels of foreign trade, and a sharp fall in GNP. The details of the depression are set out in Table IV.

The course of the depression and the reasons for its severity were determined to a large extent by the nature of its causes. On the one hand the fall-off in demand, both at home and abroad, produced a contraction of industrial investment and a lowering of prices. On the other the difficulties of the international financial system deepened the depression, making it a far more catastrophic event than might otherwise have been the case. The international economic crisis affected all the main industrial powers, but it affected Germany with a particular severity. The first reason for this was the sharp decline in lending to Germany already noted. Then there was the problem of the withdrawal of funds already loaned. This was a much more serious problem. In 1931, with the German economy showing no sign of revival and international confidence at a low ebb, the withdrawal of funds became a flood. By the end of 1931 over 6.5 billion marks had been withdrawn from Germany or sent out by German investors seeking greater security.

The crisis at an international level came to a head in June and July 1931, triggered off by the international reaction to the German proposal for a customs union with Austria. Throughout June funds were hastily withdrawn from the German banks. The traditionally cautious attitude of the German banks had been undermined during the 1920s by the general availability of foreign money. By 1929 the ratio of capital to deposits, which had been

1:3 or 1:4 in 1914 was as high as 1:20 [103: *113*]. Almost 50 per cent of the deposits held by the beginning of the recession was foreign money. Under these circumstances any sudden withdrawal of funds would be disastrous both for the banks' own liquidity and for the balance of payments. As the foreign creditors increased demands for repayment in the middle of 1931, the banks began to call in loans, as far as they could, from the firms to whom the money had been lent. It was at this point that the other interested parties intervened. In the United States President Hoover announced on 20 June a moratorium on all international capital movements. Five days later a loan of 420 million marks was paid to Germany to cope with the emergency. But by then the crisis had already deepened too much. It made little difference that the French refused to ratify the moratorium until 6 July. In the wake of the collapse of the Austrian banking system the first large German bank, the Darmstädter und Nationalbank, collapsed on 13 July [103: *111–15*; 23: *266*].

The German government adopted two lines of approach to the financial collapse. The first had been to press from 1930 onwards for international co-operation in solving the economic crisis and a reduction in the level of protective tariffs and discriminatory regulations that had been established by other countries as a defence against the depression. The effect of these protectionist measures had been to accelerate the decline of world trade, to reduce demand for German goods abroad and hence to reduce Germany's ability to pay the war-related debts. Although German complaints received a sympathetic hearing, there was little positive, international co-operation to restore the world market to health [47]. The other line of approach was to take over the banking system, at least for the duration of the crisis, and to try to control as far as possible the flows of capital, the foreign exchange market and the structure of internal credit. Compelled by necessity both the banks and the government co-operated to replace private banking and financial institutions with a system of public regulation and control.

The banking crisis elicited the first positive efforts on the part of the government, or private business for that matter, to alleviate the worst effects of the depression. And it was perhaps significant that such efforts were not made until the German economy seemed on the point of complete collapse. To many historians since the depression the actions of the German government throughout the crisis have had the appearance of shutting the stable door well after the horse has bolted. In the light of the fact that the crisis was so much more severe than earlier crises, there is a strong case for arguing that the German government, and particularly the government of Chancellor Brüning which took office in March 1930, should have used government powers to reduce the impact of the depression. Policies of lower interest rates, increased government expenditure (by deficit if necessary) and devaluation to make German exports more competitive have all been canvassed by economists and economic historians as policies that would have combated the crisis and perhaps have avoided the triumph of fascism in 1933.

The main problem with such an argument is that it takes little account of the historical circumstances with which the German government was faced. In the first place it was by no means clear until the sharp financial crisis of 1931 that the depression was any different from earlier depressions. The short downswing in 1926 had produced a level of industrial production and employment lower than that in Germany at the end of 1930. Borchardt has argued that there were signs of recovery in Germany and in the world economy in the early months of 1931 that would have suggested to any government at the time that the purging process of recession was over and extraordinary policies therefore unnecessary [13: *145–7*]. In the second place the government and states in Germany already played an important part in the German economy before 1929 and there was widespread resistance in the private sector to the further extension of government intervention in the economy, as there was in Britain and France as well. The laissez-faire attitudes of many German businessmen and politicians were not a product of prejudice or self-interest alone, but were the product of a genuine belief that there was no other way to weather a recession but through traditional, deflationary means. To have done otherwise would have been to fly in the face of prevailing economic theory and political inclination.

Given these circumstances it is by no means clear that historians' remedies for the problems of the depression in Germany would have been recognised as necessary by contemporaries or would even have worked. Low interest rates were unlikely to have had the necessary effect since there were many other factors affecting entrepreneurial decisions in 1930–2. Moreover high interest rates were deemed necessary in a situation where German creditworthiness and international liquidity were high priorities. A higher level of government spending by itself would have alleviated some of the unemployment, but would have produced consternation among the conservative politicians and financiers abroad who were in a position to influence the course of German economic policy. Such a policy, if combined with devaluation of the mark, would have been regarded at the time as dangerously inflationary. In Germany the political effect of pursuing policies alleged to be inflationary would have been disastrous for Brüning. Nor was devaluation the answer. It would not necessarily have helped Germany's balance of trade (which was already in surplus by 1931) or balance of payments (since it would have made payments abroad more expensive) and it gave no guarantee that demand for German goods would revive given the general nature of the trading and financial crisis. To have worked it would have required other countries to stop devaluing competitively and to reduce tariffs at the same time, which they were clearly unwilling to do. By contrast, a comparatively over-valued mark did have the advantages both of making it progressively easier to pay off international debt and of reducing import prices, particularly of raw materials. In the political and economic context of the depression all policies carried advantages and disadvantages. There was no easy Keynesian answer to the crisis.

For the German government, faced with the uncertainties surrounding any less orthodox economic policy, it made much more sense to do as little as was necessary. The safe option chosen was deflation. This was the prevailing economic orthodoxy and it satisfied conservative political circles at home. It was the way almost all governments responded to economic crisis. There can be little doubt that this contributed, as did international economic problems, to deepening the recession. But it should not be exaggerated. In 1931 total budget expenditures fell from 13.1 billion marks in 1930 to 11.3 billion at current prices, a fall of 13 per cent. In real terms the fall was only 9.8 per cent. As a percentage of GNP government expenditure was actually higher in

1931 than in 1930. Even in 1932, with a sharper fall in the real value of government expenditure, the level was higher as a proportion of GNP than in any year of the 1920s. The deflation decrees, which began with the decree of 7 July 1930 ordering a 10 per cent reduction of all wages, prices, rents and profits, and continued throughout 1931 and 1932, were designed to have the positive effect of lowering variable costs for industry. High wages and artificially high cartel prices were cited by many businessmen as an explanation for declining profits and business crisis. The deflation was designed to lower these costs to compensate for the high cost of capital. The government also allowed an unpublicised 'backdoor' reflation in 1931 by permitting the Reichsbank to reduce the ratio of gold to note issue from the 40 per cent agreed in the bank law of 1924 to only 10 per cent in January 1932 [51: *316–20*; 59: *107–8*]. It was kept secret for fear of the effects on domestic and foreign opinion.

What the government did not do was introduce public policies of credit creation or stimulate demand artificially. Stolper, among others, has suggested that expansionary, proto-Keynesian policies were not pursued because no such alternative policy was ever seriously proposed [103: *116–18*]. This was not the case. Meister and Nicholls have both shown that alternative economic strategies were formulated and widely disseminated, even in government circles [71; 79]. Throughout 1931 and 1932 an active debate was carried on over the appropriate economic strategy for Germany to adopt. Opposed to the orthodox laissez-faire economists were those such as Wilhelm Röpke, whose reports for the Brauns Commission on unemployment in 1931 stressed the need for a 'first spark' (*Initialzündung*) in the form of state investment programmes to get industrial production going again [88: *430–5*]. Garvy has demonstrated that German economists were familiar by the 1920s with many of the ideas developed later in Keynes' *General Theory*. He argues that the theoretical base developed by economists such as Ernst Wagemann or Heinrich Dräger, whose works were published in 1932, could have provided the government with the foundation for a reflationary policy [37: *397–8*]. Efforts were even made to recruit Keynes to help persuade the government to adopt a programme of public works, tax concessions and expanded industrial investment, but Keynes declined to help on the curious ground that his German was not good enough. The problem faced by those favouring unorthodox expansionary policies was their lack of political influence. This was not just because Brüning himself now seems to have been opposed to schemes of deficit-financing on theoretical grounds, but also because the champions of a new economic theory were of junior rank or were outsiders like Röpke or Woytinsky with no political power base [102: *103–5*].

This fact throws into sharp relief the central answer to the question of why the German government failed to respond to the depression with Keynesian or quasi-Keynesian policies. The main factors governing policy-choice were not economic but political. Much recent research in Germany has been concerned to show how economic choices were governed by political pressures and constraints, particularly in domestic politics rather than foreign policy, on which more traditional explanations have been based. Had the factors been simply economic it might have been possible to devise the necessary policies for economic revival. But they were not. Brüning's capacity for action during the depression was crucially governed by political questions. In the first place, as Brüning himself would later argue, German policy was dependent on the attitude and actions of other powers. This is a point that needs to be re-emphasised; historians have been too ready to relegate it to the sidelines. Reparations required that Germany be seen to be behaving responsibly in economic affairs. So, too, did the high level of foreign debt that bound Germany much more than other powers to more scrupulous trade and financial policies. A high premium was placed upon confidence in Germany's creditworthiness as a precondition for any renegotiation of the Versailles settlement, a fact of increasing importance in 1929–31 with the growing strength of French finances and the possibility of retaliation against German default. Some of these arguments may seem hard to sustain in the light of the Nazis' later willingness to ignore international agreements and financial arrangements, but nevertheless the evidence shows overwhelmingly that international political considerations governed a large part of German policy-making in the central years of the depression.

Of equal importance however, were questions of domestic politics. In the first place all political parties were agreed on the need to defend the currency at all costs. Deflationary policies guaranteed that there would be no repeat of the disastrous inflation of 1923. The link in people's minds between unorthodox economic policies and inflationary crisis may well have been a false one, but it nevertheless acted as a major psychological constraint in any discussion of new ways to fight the crisis. It is significant that not even the German Social Democratic Party (SPD) or the trade unions were prepared to do anything that threatened to upset economic 'stability'. The SPD, rather like the British Labour Party, failed conspicuously to approach the depression with any positive proposals. On the one hand they were persuaded by Hilferding that Marxists should defend the currency as vigorously as anyone because of the threat that inflation represented to the ordinary working man; and on the other they argued that they should do nothing that undermined rising real wages. Since prices were falling faster than wages for those in employment, and since the bulk of SPD votes came from those still with jobs, the socialist leaders argued, with a remarkable degree of circularity, that they should do nothing that jeopardised the short-term gain in real income [115: *462–72*]. This position, and that of the conservative parties, was strengthened by the unfortunate fact that unorthodox economic policy was associated with the political extremes, with the German Communist Party and the Nazis. Both parties, from different angles, stressed the need for state policies to combat unemployment, to cut Germany off much more from the effects of the world market, while opposing deflationary and orthodox economic policies. In the political circumstances of 1931 and 1932 it seemed to many that to pursue expansionary economic policies was to lurch into radicalism.

This political division was complicated even more by what German historians have come to call interest-group politics [38; 99; 110]. It was not only parties but also large-scale business and agrarian organisations that were involved in policy-making. This dimension was more important in Germany than elsewhere in Europe because of the considerable degree of social power and political influence exercised by business leaders and the larger landholders. The obvious feature of interest-group politics is that each group has different interests. Industry itself was roughly divided between the export sector and the heavy industrial groups.

Agriculture, because of the increasing need for protection, came to identify more with the latter. The export sector wanted efforts to revive trade, international co-operation and cheap raw materials. Heavy industry and agriculture wanted a more closed economy, protection and guaranteed cartel and agricultural prices [1]. They were agreed that efforts should be made to reduce wage costs, while maintaining artificially high prices for food products and industrial raw materials. The divisions were not, of course, exclusive. There were large corporations engaged in export and primary production. There were smaller farmers who favoured cheaper fodder imports but restrictions on other imported food. But there was a general expectation that the government should not embark on any policy in favour of one group at the expense of the rest. In the face of so many conflicting interests any government had to tread warily. Brüning hoped to strike the right balance between interest groups, parties and foreign creditors by adopting the economic policy that divided them least. In the deepening recession of the winter of 1931–2, with the prospect of a settlement of war debts getting closer, the government determined to do nothing but hang on in the grim expectation of improvement. In May 1932 the German Minister of Labour announced gloomily that there seemed 'no possibility whereby the political authorities might overcome the existing difficulties' [102: *106*]. The Brüning government lacked the political imagination to overcome the political constraints, and was able to use such constraints as a justification for economic timidity. Yet given the way in which economic and political life was structured during the depression, it is difficult, in the end, to see how Brüning could have behaved otherwise. The strength of the interest groups he faced was amply demonstrated by the fact that leading agrarian political circles were able to bring pressure to bear on President Hindenburg to dismiss Brüning in May 1932 because of his unfavourable attitude to the large aristocratic estates.

The irony of Brüning's dismissal was that circumstances were on the point of a sudden change. Even though reparations formed only part of the problem, the outcome of the Lausanne Conference in June 1932 was a victory for the German government's painstaking efforts to reduce the burden of war debt on Germany. Secondly, as orthodox economists had expected, the depression began to show signs of coming to an end in the summer of 1932. The output of producer goods turned up in the second quarter of 1932, that of consumer durables in the third quarter. Profits began to rise as a proportion of industrial income, while costs fell far enough to restore some measure of business confidence. There was an important change in the prevailing attitude to government intervention. While many businessmen continued to resist pressure for more government intervention, the very intensity of the crisis, and the mounting fear of political extremism, inclined both politicians and businessmen to accept more state initiative in helping the economy to recover. Even the Brüning government had drawn up preliminary plans for work-creation projects. Given such preparations, and the knowledge that economic conditions had now reached their lowest ebb, circumstances were ripe for some departure from the negative policies of the depression years. How great a departure continued to depend upon political circumstances.

3

The nature of the recovery

There is no general agreement about when the economic recovery began in Germany. Some indices show an early upward movement in the middle of 1932, but unemployment peaked slightly later and in the early months of 1933 there was a growing fear that the optimistic signs of the previous year, like those of 1931, had been a mirage. The *Institut für Konjunkturforschung* compared the period with the prolonged depression of 1875–95. Only by the second quarter of 1933 did it become clear that a more general improvement was taking place. By the end of that year the index of industrial production (1928 = 100) stood at 66, seven points higher than in 1932, and unemployment fell by over two million between March 1933 and March 1934. By 1935 GNP in real terms had reached the level of 1928. The peak figure of the 1920s for industrial production was reached by 1936, that for employment by 1937. By 1938 the economy was entering a period of growth well above the level of 1913 for the first time since the end of the war. The figures were not all that remarkable by international standards. Madison has shown that almost all Germany's neighbours and major competitors had a higher growth record between 1913 and 1938 [66: *138–48*]. But the recovery was remarkable given the particular circumstances of the German economy at the beginning of the 1930s. A combination of structural problems and political instability made it seem likely to many contemporaries that the German economy would not be able to revive at all except through a lengthy and painful economic cleansing process. In fact the German economy grew at a faster rate during the 1930s than the world economy as a whole, in the attempt to 'catch up' with the level of growth achieved elsewhere before 1929. The record of the recovery is set out in Table V.

Table V *Statistics of recovery in Germany 1932–8*

	1928	1932	1933	1934	1935	1936	1937	1938
GNP (by RM)	89.5	57.6	59.1	66.5	74.4	82.6	93.2	104.5
GNP (1928 prices)	89.5	71.9	73.7	83.7	92.3	101.2	114.2	126.2
National income (bn RM)	75.4	45.2	46.5	52.8	59.1	65.8	73.8	82.1
Industrial production (1928 = 100)	100	58	66	83	96	107	117	122
Unemployment (m.)		1.4	5.6	4.8	2.7	2.2	1.6	0.9	0.4

Source: [42: 277].

There have been many kinds of explanation for the revival. Some have centred narrowly on one factor – work-creation schemes or rearmament are among the favourites – but as more research unfolds it has become clear that there is no single or simple answer. To some extent the revival was fuelled by the normal operation of the business cycle, independent of state initiative. James has argued that this was the case in the early stages of recovery, before state policies had begun to take effect. There was a minor consumer boom in 1933/4 made evident in the rapid increases in inventory investment – restocking after the decline produced by the slump – particularly among small businesses [52]. By 1932 prices and wages had reached rock-bottom and the prospect of re-starting production with much reduced costs restored some of the battered confidence of the business community. The final solution to the reparations issue in 1932 provided another psychological boost. The consumer industries revived rapidly in 1933. The recovery, according to James, was 'spontaneous' rather than manufactured by the state.

Clearly the recovery did owe something to the business cycle, whose upturn the new Hitler government was able to exploit to its advantage. But such an argument sits uneasily with the view that the Weimar economy was weakened by structural deficiencies and political conflict. It is unlikely that a spontaneous recovery in the business cycle in the gloomy world context of 1933 would have solved those structural problems; at best it might have produced a recovery that peaked well short of full employment. There were few who wanted or expected the state to remain economically neutral. The recovery was conditioned by political circumstances and sustained by state initiative.

Some historians have gone so far as to suggest that the new regime developed a coherent alternative economic system within which the recovery could be orchestrated. Both Barkai and Volkmann see the economic interventionism of the Nazi government in the context of a German *dirigiste* tradition. The recession exposed the weakness of the liberal market economy and turned German economists and politicians to the idea of state management of the economy and relative isolation from the world market [9; 110]. Barkai has argued, much along the lines of earlier economists, that to operate the system the regime constructed an institutional framework and a set of policy instruments designed to achieve the ideological re-ordering of the economy on interventionist, autarkic lines. A great many academic economists, Nazi and non-Nazi, had argued for just such a change to the system well before 1933 [110: *169–93*].

Such views certainly matched the economic nationalism of the Nazi movement and its leaders, and their anti-liberal, anti-capitalist outlook. Whether their ambitions amounted to a new economic system, ideologically determined, remains a subject of debate. There were too many ideological divisions and institutional rivalries to be confident of the coherence of the Nazi economic alternative. The continuities evident in economic policy between Weimar and the Third Reich suggest that January 1933 was a less significant turning point in economic strategy than was once thought.

Nonetheless the arrival of Hitler did bring a clear political change. The new regime promised to end the social and political instability of the last Weimar years, which the business community welcomed. Fears about the radical character of the Nazi movement subsided as Hitler made it clear that he wanted no economic experiments. The destruction of the trade unions in May 1933 and the freeze on wage rates also met business interests. The regime's energetic and much-publicised re-employment campaign simplified the political arguments of the recession period and showed the wider German public that the regime was committed to what they perceived to be the central economic issue [81]. The new government also reflected the popular mood of economic nationalism, both in its desire to cut Germany off from unhealthy dependence on the world economy and in the pursuit of domestic sources of recovery. Above all, the change in government raised the expectations of producers and consumers beyond the grim realities of the recession. The political climate reinforced, or may even have caused, the popular conviction that revival was a possibility, however muted the initial intervention of the Nazi state may have been.

The economic nationalism of the regime was expressed in the changing relationship of Germany with the world economy. In the 1920s this relationship left Germany highly vulnerable to sudden changes in the world market and to foreign confidence in German prospects. The end of reparations in 1932 and the cessation of foreign lending removed two potentially unstable elements. The new regime rejected any idea of reviving reparation payments and effectively defaulted on much of its international debt. In the context of worldwide protectionism Germany became willy-nilly more isolated from the world market. During 1933 and 1934 Germany's own trade and payments abroad became subject to state supervision. In September 1934 comprehensive controls over foreign transactions were established in the so-called 'New Plan' drawn up by Hjalmar Schacht, President of the Reichsbank and Minister of Economics. Imports could only be brought in under licence; capital could not be moved freely abroad; foreign earnings in Germany were kept in blocked accounts, to be spent only on German goods and services. Where feasible the government negotiated barter agreements with other traders in order to secure essential supplies of food and raw materials. Not surprisingly, foreign lending became insignificant in the 1930s. Only Britain maintained credit lines of any size to Germany, in order to secure German machinery and equipment [35].

There was a price to pay for protectionism. German trade, like world trade, collapsed during the slump. By 1933 exports were only 39 per cent of the level in 1928. This situation improved little during the 1930s. Exports were higher in value in 1932 than in 1938 (see Table VI for details of German foreign trade). The

Table VI *German trade statistics 1928–38*

	1928	1932	1933	1934	1935	1936	1937	1938
Exports								
(bn RM)	12.3	5.7	4.9	4.2	4.3	4.8	5.9	5.3
Imports								
(bn RM)	14.0	4.7	4.2	4.5	4.2	4.2	5.5	5.4
Balance of								
trade	−1.7	1.0	0.7	−0.3	0.1	0.6	0.4	−0.1

Source: [59: *483*].

improved terms of trade produced by falls in food and commodity prices, the relatively high value of the mark, and the general crisis of world trade and payments all militated against a revival based on exports. Trade was the subject of negotiation between protectionist states. By 1938 over 50 per cent of German trade was covered by bilateral agreements. In 1936 the government embarked on an extensive programme of import-substitution because of the poor state of world trade and fears of economic discrimination and blockade, particularly in time of war. In October 1936 the Four Year Plan was announced. The plan was to provide Germany with supplies of iron ore, fuel oil, rubber and textiles produced from home supplies or from chemical substitutes. Although the plan had a clear military purpose, there were also pressures for self-sufficiency both from those domestic industries which hoped to profit from the import-substitution programme, and from the distorted character of the world market which provided only limited opportunities for trade growth.

The self-sufficiency drive coincided with efforts to shift the direction of German trade towards central and eastern Europe, which many regarded as both a natural and more secure area for German trade expansion. But there were limits even to trade in eastern Europe, as recent research has shown. Contemporaries greatly exaggerated the importance of eastern Europe for the German economy, until, that is, the onset of military conquest. Kaiser has argued that eastern Europe was itself industrialising in the 1930s with the help of western capital and did not want to be drawn into a permanent, semi-colonial, relationship with Germany [53: *141–2*]. Throughout the 1930s the countries of eastern

Europe fought shy of close links, leaving Germany with trading deficits with almost all her eastern neighbours for most of the 1930s [77: *398–403*]. German trade continued to be predominantly with western Europe, Latin America and the Middle East. Britain was both the most important creditor of and the largest trader with Germany by 1938. The Balkan states bought only 6.9 per cent of German exports in 1935 and by 1938, despite growing political pressure, this figure had risen only to 11 per cent.

There was another disadvantage in Germany's growing isolation from the world market and the protection of German agriculture. The full effect of the fall in world prices, particularly of foodstuffs and other raw materials, was not passed on to the German consumer as it was in other advanced economies. In Britain the motor for expansion in the 1930s was provided by cheap imports, a consequent rise in real income and a growing demand for home-produced manufactured goods. In response to this increased demand for industrial goods further gains were made in improving technology and organisation to meet the demand. The rise in productivity then stimulated further demand growth. In this way home demand provided the kind of stimulus that had been provided by the growth of trade before 1913 or 1929.

The question that immediately arises is where did the extra demand come from in Germany if not from abroad, or from increase in real income produced by cheaper imports and food? Export growth had been vital to the Weimar economy; how was this gap to be made good in an economy where domestic demand had grown only slowly even in the buoyant years of the mid-1920s? The first thing to observe about the pattern of demand in the German economy after 1933 is the shift from demand for consumer goods to demand for capital goods and industrial raw materials. In other words, the expansion of domestic demand did not depend so much on the growth of consumption, as it did in the 1920s, but more on the growth of heavy industry and construction. Table VII shows the changing relationship between consumer-goods and capital-goods production between 1933 and 1938. The second feature is the high level of government expenditure. The main explanation for increases in demand lies with the increase in public investment and state policies designed directly or indirectly to stimulate demand. How much effect such policies had will be

Table VII *Relative growth of producer and consumer goods in Germany 1929–38 (1928 = 100)*

	1929	1932	1938
Total production	110.9	58.7	124.7
Capital goods	103.2	45.7	135.9
Consumer goods	98.5	78.1	107.8
Pig-iron	113.8	33.4	157.3
Machinery	103.8	40.7	147.7
Chemicals	91.8	50.9	127.0
Textiles	92.4	79.2	107.5
Household furniture	104.2	69.6	113.6

Source: [60: *352*].

discussed in greater detail in Chapter 4. Government programmes of construction and rearmament were also responsible for shifting the emphasis of growth from consumer industries to the other major sectors of the economy.

Some government policies, it is true, were designed to stimulate consumer spending as well. This was true of agricultural policy. Farquharson has shown that a feature of the late 1920s and the depression years was the decline of agricultural prices and the relative increase in taxation and debt charges for farmers. Some efforts were made in 1932 to improve the situation, but not until the Nazis came to power, partly on the basis of the peasant vote, were measures promoted to increase prices for farmers by granting a guaranteed minimum price, and to reduce the burden of taxation and interest. These payments represented 22 per cent of the value of farm output in 1932. By 1934/5 they stood at 13 per cent. Agrarian incomes increased by 17 per cent in the first year of recovery, 16 per cent in the second, while incomes for all sectors of the economy expanded in those periods by only 6 per cent and 12 per cent. By 1934–5 the agricultural surplus was almost 50 per cent higher than it had been in 1928–9 [31: *66–7*]. Farmers bought tractors and fertilisers with the new money, providing in turn a stimulus to the manufacturing sectors. It is difficult to indicate exactly what impact the increase in agricultural incomes had on the growth of demand, for some of the new income was used for saving and debt repayment, but agricultural revival was an important feature of the early years of recovery, and deserves more attention than it has received.

Demand was stimulated among small businessmen as well. Many had been hit particularly severely by the depression, with the aggregate income of small businesses declining from 20 billion marks in 1926 to only 11 billion by 1932. Government spending policies, directed once again in favour of a group sympathetic to the Nazi government, played an important part, whether through construction, rearmament or road-building, in providing contracts for small firms. There was a deliberate emphasis on encouraging small workshops to modernise by buying subsidised tools and equipment which in turn provided a further stimulus to the machinery and building materials industries. Other middle-class groups, many of whom had increased levels of savings by the mid-1930s compared with the post-inflation period, provided a source of demand for consumer durables such as cars, whose output trebled between 1933 and 1938. Finally demand increased, as in other advanced countries, through the continuous changes in the structure of the workforce away from low-paid, unskilled jobs to more skilled or white-collar employment, and through the significant shift from unemployment to re-employment, part cause, part effect, of the increase in demand.

However, there are serious objections to any demand-based analysis of the German recovery. The 'spontaneous' recovery detected by James in 1933 depended a good deal on state incentives, either in the form of tax concessions (for new car owners, for example), or in terms of direct subsidies (for house repair and household goods). Consumer industries benefited from the scheme of marriage loans set up in the summer of 1933, in which the state offered loans of up to 1,000 RM in value in the form of certificates to be spent on furniture and household goods. By the end of 1933 183,000 loans had been taken up, pumping over 1 billion marks into a sector dominated by small businesses [82: 49]. The revival of the consumer sectors produced by these state schemes soon petered out. Private consumption and the level of consumer industry output responded slowly to the recovery, despite the achievement of full employment in 1938. Although Klein has argued that per capita consumption reached the levels of 1929 by 1938, this achievement has to be set against an increase in real GNP per capita of 31 per cent and in industrial output of 22 per cent over the level of 1929 [57: *11*]. The increase in consumer demand was well below the overall increase in economic activity, a fact reflected in the declining share of wage income in the national product.

The level of private consumption was influenced by the slow growth of real earnings during the 1930s. The regime, as Siegel has argued, pegged wages at depression rates, and turned a blind eye to employers who undercut the official levels. Many of the re-employed worked on work-creation schemes, or in some form of labour service, where there was little cash pay at all. Average earnings were actually lower in 1933 and 1934 than in the last depression year, 1932 [96: *9–13*]. Changes in productivity were used to boost profits and investments rather than raise wage rates. Expressed as either wage-rates or earnings, the real value of incomes peaked in 1929–30 and declined thereafter. Real earnings only regained the 1929 level in 1941 under pressure of wartime labour scarcity (see Table VIII for details on wages and consumption). Some account must also be taken of the declining quality of goods as firms substituted poorer materials for those no longer imported, and of the effects on take-home pay produced by higher levels of taxation and compulsory levies. Far from pursuing, inadvertently or otherwise, a Keynesian strategy in the 1930s, the Nazi government controlled the growth of private consumption by redistributing income to profits and investment or to the state. Such policies reinforced the effect of debt repayment after 1933 observed by Svennilson, which shifted much of the increased income away from those who might have spent it on consumer goods to those with a greater interest in taking up government loans or investing in industry [104: *39–51*]. The government was able to use these funds for its own purposes, particularly for the large capital-projects undertaken by public authorities, and for war preparation.

The slow growth of domestic consumer demand and the collapse of exports throws into sharp relief the importance of investment, and government investment in particular, in explaining the recovery. This was a critical variable, for it was the sharp fall in foreign investment, and subsequently of investment as a whole, that created such havoc in the economy during the depression.

Table VIII *Real wages in Germany 1928–38*

	Real wages (1913–14 = 100)	Money wages (1913–14 = 100)	Real earnings (1925–9 = 100)	Wages as % of NI	Private consumption as % of NI
1928	110	168	106	62	71
1930	122	180	114	–	–
1931	125	171	106	–	–
1932	120	144	91	64	83
1933	119	140	87	63	81
1934	116	140	88	62	76
1935	114	140	91	61	71
1936	112	140	93	59	64
1937	112	140	96	58	62
1938	112	141	101	57	59

Source: [17: *331, 362*; 85: *438*; 66: *438*; 103: *150*].

The high rate of interest throughout the depression period and the poor financial position of the banks made it difficult and unattractive to acquire new funds. By 1931 large-scale disinvestment had set in in the private sector. By 1932 public investment fell to a third of the level of 1928. Most historians have laid special emphasis, and rightly so, on the revival of investment as an explanation for the German recovery. In 1928 gross investment was 18 per cent of national income; by 1936 it was 26 per cent and by 1938 27.5 per cent.

Much of the new investment came from the state. Some 45 per cent of gross investment between 1933 and 1938 was paid for by government funds. This was the kind of strategy that many German economists had demanded in 1932 as the only way to combat unemployment and regenerate the economy. In fact the Nazi government went much further than expected in maintaining high levels of state expenditure and public investment throughout the 1930s. By 1938 state spending accounted for 33 per cent of GNP as against only 17 per cent in 1932. A large part of the later spending was directed towards war purposes and the building up of domestic synthetic production. It was financed in a number of different ways, partly through taxation (which remained at a high level throughout the period), partly through deficit-financing and a large increase in the government debt from 13.9 billion marks at the end of 1933 to 41.7 billion at the end of 1938. By 1938 the money supply was 70 per cent greater than in 1933, and 45 per cent greater than in 1929, the peak of the earlier revival [58: *135*]. To ensure that the money was spent in the way that they wanted, the Nazi government instituted a complex system of controls over the money market and direct investment. As a result of these controls industry was compelled to maintain high levels of internal investment from undistributed profits. The freedom to issue shares for industrial expansion was effectively removed and all new share issues required government sanction. Private share issues had totalled 9 billion marks from 1926 to 1929. From 1933 to 1938 the figure was only 2.6 billion [28: *67*].

Private investment in general revived much more slowly than public. The incentives for different sectors were very uneven. On the one hand some of heavy industry, particularly iron and steel, suffered from over-capacity based on the large investment drive of the 1926–8 period. The problem here was not a lack of investment but how to utilise existing capacity. Other sectors in which investment was lacking were, on the other hand, discriminated against by government policy and were unable to get the capital they needed. This particularly affected the consumer industries. Under such conflicting economic conditions it was difficult for private business confidence to be fully restored and, where private investment did occur in significant volume, it was in those sectors, such as the motor industry, which the government had singled out for special concessions [82: *78–80*]. Under these circumstances public investment, or private investment under government regulation, came to play a key part in the expansion and restructuring of the domestic economy (see Table IX).

It might be expected that such a high level of investment, directed as much of it was by the state, would have produced an economy in which the engine of growth was once again technological change. Landes and Svennilson both emphasise the importance of productivity growth and the 'new industries' for explaining what growth there was in the inter-war period [61; 104]. In the German case this would be a mistake. High investment levels did not lead to a corresponding increase in industrial productivity. Between 1929 and 1938 the average increase was 1.3 per cent, a quarter of the levels achieved in the 1950s. This was

Table IX *Public and private investment in Germany 1928–38*

	1928	1932	1933	1934	1935	1936	1937	1938
Total public investment (bn RM)	6.6	2.2	2.5	4.6	6.4	8.1	8.4	10.3
Total private investment (bn RM)	9.7	0.3	3.2	4.7	7.2	9.2	10.5	12.2
Total all investment (bn RM)	16.3	2.5	5.7	9.3	13.6	17.3	18.9	22.5
Private share issues (bn RM)	2.5	–	0.1	0.1	0.3	0.6	0.7	0.9
Net private industrial investment* (bn RM)	1.0	0.8	0.7	−0.2	0.3	0.7	n.a.	n.a.
All net investment as a % of NI	9.3	−**	−**	5.3	8.8	11.5	13.1	15.7

Source: [28: *67*; 57: *255–6*; 64: *23, 38*].
* Excluding inventories. ** Negative net investment.

due partly to the labour-intensive nature of many of the revival policies, and partly to the absence of a sufficient market pressure on firms to improve methods, in the form either of vigorous consumer demand or of higher profits, both of which were restricted by the state. Because of the nature of government controls and numerous government contracts, there was less incentive to be competitive or efficient.

Public investment and spending policies of sufficiently large scale lay at the centre of the recovery and must remain the primary explanation. There was not enough scope for export-led growth, or for growth based on the buoyant expansion of consumer demand, for both economic circumstances and government policy dictated otherwise. It was left to state expenditure to generate large increases in employment and income. How the money was disbursed and with what effect is the subject of the next chapter. To be effective in the conditions of the early 1930s, state policy had to be directed not only towards investment but towards most of the variables at work in the economy. Increasingly the government was compelled to control prices, wages, private investment, the banks and all aspects of foreign trade. All of these controls operating within the context of investment-led growth help to explain the scope and speed of the revival.

4
Government and recovery

The German economic recovery was an example of state-led growth in what was still ostensibly a capitalist economy. This is not to suggest that recovery could only occur under state direction. Some level of recovery would have been achieved without state help. But the characteristic features of the revival – the control of trade, the intervention in the capital market, high levels of investment and a rapid return to full employment – were dictated by the strategies of the regime, not the pressures of the market-place.

There was nothing new about the state taking initiatives in the economy. Stolper and Barkai have both demonstrated that the growing intervention of the state in economic affairs from 1931 onwards was very much in the tradition of German state policy [9; 103]. Yet it would be difficult to deny that Hitler's advent to power in January 1933 did represent in important respects a shift away from the mixed economy of the Weimar Republic. The Nazis approached the German economy with no definite plan, certainly nothing like the Soviet predictive planning of the 1930s. They sought some way of providing a conspicuous solution to unemployment as a way to stabilise the regime politically. If we cannot quite believe Hitler's own claim to have spent sleepless nights trying to find a way to solve the question of 'Bread and Work', it seems clear enough that Hitler realised that his mandate rested on finding an economic strategy to end the recession. On Hitler's long-term plans there is less certainty. He regarded the economy instrumentally, as a sphere which would ultimately serve other ends – the re-militarisation of Germany and the achievement of hegemony in Europe. There was a strong economic core to his strategic and geo-political outlook: to survive economically the

German people needed *Lebensraum* (living space). For Hitler, recovery was a stepping stone to a brighter economic future when Germany ruled a Eurasian empire.

This broader, ill-defined ambition was little in evidence in the early years of the regime. Recovery was the immediate priority. Hitler was prepared to give the responsibility for creating this recovery to the bankers, civil servants and industrialists who had the expertise. It did not matter that the leading Nazis themselves knew very little about economics; what mattered was their ability to recruit and discipline those who did. The Nazis were prepared (in fact they believed it to be an essential part of their economic strategy) to coerce any group or individual who stood in the way of their political, economic and racial ambitions. 'The public interest before selfish interest' was the slogan used to justify the destruction of the labour organisations in May 1933, the aryanisation of Jewish businesses, and the harassment of individual businessmen like Hugo Junkers, who refused to produce warplanes for Göring and found his business nationalised. Even Schacht, Minister of Economics from 1934 to 1937 and responsible for much of the early recovery policy, was not indispensable and ended up in a concentration camp.

Because of this reliance on the existing expertise of business and civil service, it was unnecessary at first to create new institutions of economic management. The existing state structure was used for the purpose. Many of the controls and regulations instituted were, in turn, borrowed from previous regimes which had used them as instruments in an emergency. Indeed the government fought shy of appearing to control the economy too closely in order not to alienate the business world. They hoped that revival might be generated through private business initiative on the basis of a 'first spark' provided by the state. In fact, as Erbe argued in a Keynesian interpretation of the Nazi recovery published in 1958, private initiative did not respond vigorously and the 'first spark' turned, as Hitler had perhaps always intended, into a permanent involvement in the economy [28: 69]. There was a difference here between liberal recovery policies such as those in Britain and the United States which were designed to stimulate the early stages of a recovery which would then become self-sustaining and reduce the need for state intervention, and those of the Nazi regime. In

Germany the economy travelled in the opposite direction, moving from a cautious introduction of state policies in 1933 to a complete system of controls – what Neumann called the 'command economy' – established by 1938 [78: *240–96*]. The secret behind the Nazi economic revival was not merely proto-Keynesian spending policies but the whole 'package' of controls, all of them inter-dependent, all of them necessary to achieve what the Nazis wanted from the economy. Without such a 'package' the economy might not have recovered to the extent that it did or in the way that Hitler's future war plans dictated. State intervention meant attacking the structural problems of the economy on a broad front and not at one particular point.

The central feature of Nazi policy was, nevertheless, a programme of government spending and public investment designed to stimulate demand and expand income. The strategy adopted had a number of different features. There were policies aimed at stimulating demand indirectly through increasing purchasing power and encouraging the propensity to consume. This was done by a system of tax concessions and special grants. Tax levels were reduced for farmers, for small businesses and for heavy industry in the form of the remission of taxes already paid. The sums involved were not that great, and in the case of concessions to large-scale industry had much less effect than had been intended. The large firms used their new liquidity to repay bank debts rather than generate demand for goods and there was no guarantee that the banks would stimulate the economy with the new funds in quite the way intended [86: *256–8*]. The system of grants operated at the same time was more successful but again was of modest scope. Grants were given to newly-weds to spend on household goods and furniture, or to householders to encourage house-repair. Additional grants were given to industries to enable them to purchase machinery or to help towards the cost of hiring additional labour. Subsidies were also given for the re-employment or increased employment of domestic servants [64: *6–18*].

The indirect stimulus gave way during the course of 1933 and 1934 to a high level of direct state expenditure on industrial investment, construction and employment programmes. Indeed the indirect demand policies gave way by 1935 to policies designed to curb consumer spending in favour of higher investment activity

Table X *Government expenditure in Germany 1928–38 (bn RM)*

	1928	1929	1932	1933	1934	1935	1936	1937	1938
Total expenditure (current prices)	11.7	12.4	8.6	9.4	12.8	13.9	15.8	19.3	29.3
Total expenditure (1900 prices)	6.6	6.9	6.3	7.1	9.4	10.0	11.1	13.4	20.4
as % of GNP		14.8	15.7	17.9	18.9	22.9	22.0	22.5	24.5	33.5

Source: [3: 245].

and government-created demand. Public investment doubled between 1933 and 1934 and increased by almost 60 per cent again during 1935. In 1929 public investment was 35 per cent of gross investment; in 1935 it was 55 per cent. Total government expenditure increased in real terms by almost 300 per cent between 1933 and 1938, rising from 18 per cent to 33 per cent of GNP, as Table X shows. These were levels almost double those of the 1920s.

In addition to direct expenditure the government also sought to stimulate and control private investment activity in a number of different ways, to complement the efforts being made by the state. This control over the secondary and less direct results of government activity was carried out not only to ensure that state money was not wasted but in order to divert private initiative into the areas that the state wanted, particularly into import substitution and rearmament. The stimulation of private investment was achieved first of all through the granting of state contracts which required for their fulfilment a contribution from the individual firms and suppliers. An exception was the armaments industry in which much of the basic investment and the running costs as well were provided by the state. Secondly, concessions were made to certain firms which promised to undertake expensive projects that fitted in with the government's wider policies. That was the only way in which the Nazis could induce I. G. Farben to continue synthetic oil and rubber production in the 1930s. Another device was the restriction of profits and dividends and the compulsory retention of funds within the firm for reinvestment. Lurie has shown that the reserves thus accumulated by business were more than enough to satisfy investment needs during the upswing, while the policy of tax concessions for firms acquiring new machinery or

Table XI *National income, public spending and employment in Germany 1932–7 (1932 = 100)*

	1933	1934	1935	1936	1937
National income	103.0	116.6	129.6	145.6	163.3
Public expenditure	109.3	148.8	161.6	183.7	224.4
Employment	104.0	120.0	127.0	136.0	146.0

Source: calculated from [3: *245*; 42: *277*; 57: *251*].

extending operations with the undistributed profits encouraged them to use the money to increase fixed capital [64: *124–7*]. The result of this mixture of carrot-and-stick policies was to push private investment by 1938 to levels above public investment and to maintain an overall high level of investment activity. To ensure that private funds flowed where the government wished, it became necessary to extend more and more formal control over the banking and capital structure so that by the end of the decade it was increasingly academic to talk of a private capital market.

The result of the spending policies was a sustained rise in national income and a sharp fall in unemployment. It can be seen from Table XI that the two indices moved in step with the increase in government expenditure, with a lag to allow the increased credit to work through the system. It was Keynes who first publicised this link between government spending and an increase in income. Keynes argued that any increase in government spending would have the 'multiplier' effect of producing more income than the value of the initial expenditure because of the boost to demand and employment that it would generate. At a primary level it would encourage those who took government contracts to expand business, take on more workers and order more goods. Beyond the primary level were secondary effects as the newly employed workers spent their wages on goods; and so on. Economists debated in the 1930s what exactly the ratio of spending to income was. Keynes suggested that the ratio under average conditions was between 1:2.5 and 1:3. In Nazi Germany the ratio was substantially lower. Erbe calculated a multiplier of 1.5 – an increase in government expenditure of 32.6 billion marks and an increase in income of 52.7 billion [28: *163*]. Given the very large sums of money spent by the government the increase in income was much lower than might have been expected. Bresciani-Turroni arrived at this conclusion in his work on the Nazi economy in the 1930s and it has been confirmed subsequently [16: *7–18*]. There are a number of possible explanations. One reason for the disappointing multiplier effect was the fact that private activity did not respond as expected and government money was simply a substitute for money that would otherwise have been generated through the private capital market, and not an addition. It was also due to the relatively poor productivity performance of the 1929–38 period (of which more later), as money was poured into the less productive sectors: agriculture, armaments, roadbuilding and construction.

Nevertheless if growth was not as high as it might have been, it was high enough to achieve what the government wanted: a regenerated economy and full employment. The employment effects of the policies were more dramatic and successful than the income effects. The government was particularly anxious that employment should be increased as rapidly as possible because it had come to power on the promise to provide 'Bread and Work'. The first work-creation projects had been launched in 1932 and were expanded during 1933. Some were more useful than others in absorbing labour and they were soon eclipsed by the numbers absorbed back again into ordinary employment. In fact the most important areas for expanding employment were agriculture and the building industry, a fact that the American economist Baerwald observed in 1934. In agriculture, reorganised and assisted from the start in 1933, unemployment fell from 238,000 in March 1933 to only 66,000 a year later. In the building industry the figures were 493,000 and 107,000 respectively. Among unskilled labourers, many of whom were absorbed into the general increase in business activity, the fall in unemployment was over half a million. These three groups between them accounted for 51 per cent of the decrease in unemployment between 1933 and 1934 [5: *621*]. In addition the government sponsored schemes to increase re-employment of domestic servants and withdrew young Germans from the labour market through the compulsory Labour Service and, after 1935, through conscription. In 1934 the Labour Service projects took almost 400,000 young Germans out of the job market and into unpaid manual work, mainly on the land [82].

The novelty of the Nazi policies for expanding income and

employment lay in the way in which they were financed. If the methods are commonplace today they were unorthodox by the standards of the 1930s and inclined many economists to criticise the government for the inflationary policies that it pursued. Historians since the war, armed with Keynesian theory and common sense, have seen that the danger of a serious inflation was remote in the years of recovery from 1932 to 1936 with the existence of large unused resources and strict government control over the financial markets. The devices used were relatively simple. First and foremost the government undertook to increase the public debt. This was done, in the absence of foreign sources of funds, by borrowing on the capital market for long-term loans and by budget deficit-financing for short-term loans. The short-term financing of the deficit, that is the excess of government expenditure over government revenue, was done by issuing government bills. Much of the early financing was covered by these short-term work-creation bills, or rearmament 'Mefo'* bills which were used by government contractors to pay for what they needed. The bills were then held by the banks, by the Reichsbank or by private investors and were to be repaid by the government after five years out of the anticipated increase in tax revenue. After 1935 the government increased the amount of long-term and consolidated some of the short-term debt, compelling financial institutions to take up the new treasury bills at a lower rate of interest and without the right of re-discount at the Reichsbank which the short-term bills had carried. The advantage of the early deficit-financing was that it encouraged a rapid increase in the liquidity of the systems, for the bills could be used as a kind of currency. This reduced the dependence of industry on the banks, whose functions became progressively limited during the 1930s, and increased the velocity of circulation. The pumping of additional funds into the economy was an essential way to overcome the restrictive character of the financial system and to unclog the channels of mercantile credit which had become slowed down or blocked by the collapse of 1931 and 1932.

Other forms of finance were more conventional. Tax revenues did indeed increase as Schacht had expected (in fact taxation was

---

* Mefo = *Metallurgische-Forschungsgesellschaft* (a government holding company).

Table XII *Statistics on German finance 1928/9–1938/9 (bn RM)* *

	Government revenue	Government expenditure	Total debt	Money supply
1928–9	9.0	13.0	–	16.4
1932–3	6.6	9.2	12.3	13.4
1933–4	6.8	8.9	13.9	13.9
1934–5	8.2	12.6	15.9	15.7
1935–6	9.6	14.1	20.1	16.7
1936–7	11.4	17.3	25.8	18.1
1937–8	13.9	21.4	31.2	20.0
1938–9	17.7	32.9	41.7	23.7

* Fiscal year beginning 1 April for columns 1 and 2. End of fiscal year for column 3.
End of calendar year for column 4.
Source: [3: *245*; 28: *54, 122*; 65: *36*].

kept at very high levels throughout the 1930s), allowing the government to pay off both outstanding foreign debt and a large part of the debt contracted in the first years of recovery. The figures for government revenue, expenditure and debt are set out in Table XII. Private savings also expanded and were directed by the state into particular channels at the expense, as Poole shows, of private investment and consumption [86: *80*]. From 1933 to 1936 private savings increased by 6.9 billion marks, almost all of which went into the savings banks and into Reich finance [42: *123*]. By contrast private share issues fell from a peak of 2.5 billion marks in 1928 to an average of only 660 million marks for the years 1935–8. The bulk of all investible income after 1933 went towards financing state expenditures and not into the private sector. As a result the banks increasingly became mere intermediaries, holding government stock and helping in the job of keeping bills circulating in the way that the government wanted. The role of the traditional investment bank had been undermined by the financial crisis and replaced with investment directed largely by the state.

This discussion of how the recovery was financed begs the question of what the money was actually spent on. Implicit in this question is a further one: which of the areas of expenditure were the most important? To some extent both questions are redundant. It has already been shown that government spending and public investment explain the strength and speed of the revival and it could be argued that what the money was spent on does not matter as long as it was spent. The reason for asking more about these policies lies in the importance that many historians have attached to rearmament as the key explanation for the revival, a significance that has taken root in the popular perception of the Nazi economy. If the answer does indeed amount to rearmament, how did it generate economic growth? If not, what else was government money used for?

When Balogh was writing in the late 1930s or Erbe in the 1950s the answers seemed clear-cut. War preparation had been the intention of the government all along and war expenditures represented the bulk of government investment (over 50 per cent according to Erbe) [8: *461–5*; 28: *162–3*]. This was the chief factor in explaining growth over the period. More recent research has questioned this view, maintaining that the level of rearmament and war-related expenditures has been exaggerated. According to Milward rearmament was deliberately kept at a relatively low level because Hitler did not want to reduce civilian consumption too far and because, for the short *Blitzkrieg* campaigns that the German army appeared to pursue, a limited armament was all that was necessary [73: *Ch. I*]. In a sense both arguments are right, though not for the whole period. A detailed study of rearmament expenditure shows that it was much less important in the early years of recovery than the critics of the 1930s supposed. But it can also be shown that from 1936 onwards rearmament did assume a much greater significance, with a high level of expenditure, a general restructuring of the economy for waging war and the deliberate restraining of consumer expenditure.

The key years of economic recovery from 1932 to 1935 were years of relatively low military expenditure. From 1932–3 to 1934–5 the aggregate figure of secret budget expenditure for military purposes was 3.4 billion marks. To this should be added a figure of 2.1 billion for the special armaments bills used to finance the build-up of military industries and infrastructure. Total government expenditure over the same period was 31 billion marks. Rearmament represented some 17 per cent of total state expenditure, and only 1.3 per cent of GNP. It is difficult to see, whatever its multiplier effects, how military expenditure on its own could have accounted for the revival of business activity.

Much of the expenditure was devoted to administrative and wage costs, or to military services (in 1936 the army budget devoted only 8.6 per cent to weapons, but almost 5 per cent to horses and fodder). Military expenditure and rearmament are not the same thing. Much of the discussion of the effects of rearmament has assumed that the money was spent on industrial investment and high-quality industrial products. This was true to only a limited extent. Not until the onset of the Four Year Plan in 1936, with the large industrial projects designed to free Germany from the threat of blockade, did military preparedness make exceptional claims on the industrial economy. By 1936 the role of rearmament – either in direct supply of weapons, aircraft and equipment or in the indirect build-up of strategic industries – changed sharply. But by then the recovery was well-established.

There were also political constraints on higher levels of military expansion. The military leadership wanted a cautious build-up partly to avoid the risk of foreign intervention, and partly to ensure that the re-militarisation of Germany was carried out in a set of careful stages, under military control, rather than through a more chaotic rush for arms [24]. Business leaders were also cautious about the military programme. They too feared foreign reaction, but were also hesitant to take up extensive military investment programmes in case rearmament petered out and they were left with unutilised capacity, as they had been in 1919. The regime itself also had other priorities. There is no doubt that Hitler was committed from the outset to a policy of re-militarisation, but he did not want to sacrifice financial stability or business confidence by over-burdening the economy in the early stages of recovery. Re-employment and trade revival he regarded as a precondition for further political ambitions. Hitler also wanted to set up an ambitious programme of urban remodelling and renewal, and smother the country with new multi-lane motorways. His desire to become the *Bauherr*, the master-builder, of the new Reich competed with his plans for military revival [108]. Rearmament was one of a number of government priorities, but not the only one.

The first priority was work-creation, and this was inherited from the previous governments of von Papen and von Schleicher. The purpose of the programmes was to create direct employment through government expenditure on labour-intensive schemes of repair, maintenance and construction. Total expenditure on the schemes from 1932 to the end of 1935 was just over 5 billion marks, or slightly under 1 per cent of GNP. The direct employment created by the schemes was calculated by Grebler at 990,000 by the end of 1934, excluding house-building. A further 750,000 were at work in the winter of 1933–4 on house-repair schemes paid for in part by the government [41: *513–16*]. The short-term employment effect of the schemes was thus to absorb a large proportion of those unemployed in the late part of 1933. But the other economic effects were less than might be expected. If some writers in the 1930s were impressed by the scheme of public works, there were many at the time, and since the war, who have been sceptical about their economic significance. The first problem, as with rearmament, was the scale of expenditure. The amounts expended in the first months were very modest. The amount of extra income generated by the 1.5 billions spent by the end of 1933 cannot be accurately discovered, but the total increase in national income between 1932 and 1933 was only 1.4 billions and could only have been raised further by very much larger amounts of government spending. Work-creation may well have been responsible for preventing business activity from declining to yet lower levels in 1932 and 1933, but it is doubtful whether it provided a sufficient boost to the economy to explain the strength and speed of the revival.

The industrial strategy of the Nazis was more successful in terms of generating growth because of the linkage effects it produced and the stimulus it offered to particular areas of private business. Of the major industries affected most authors have stressed construction as the key growth area [86: *210–11*]. Other research has emphasised the role played by *Motorisierung*, the policy designed to speed up the application of the motor vehicle to the German economy [81]. In the case of motorisation the strategy was based not only on the vehicle industry itself, but on all the associated infrastructure, and particularly on the roads. What is clear is that through a number of policies of tax concessions, subsidy and direct investment both sectors were able to grow very much faster than the economy as a whole, and to drag a significant section of the rest of the industrial economy along with them. Car production was almost 50 per cent higher in 1934 than the peak reached in 1929;

expenditure on the roads (local and national) was 100 per cent higher in 1934 than in the peak year of the 1920s. The years 1932–7 were the years when the motorisation of Germany caught up with the levels achieved in other countries considerably earlier. A combination of government encouragement through propaganda and fiscal policy, increased agricultural prosperity (which encouraged farmers to buy vehicles) and a growing propensity among middle-class Germans to spend some of their growing savings on motor-cars, accounted for the buoyant growth of this particular sector.

The construction industry was similarly helped by government concessions and a high level of direct investment. Like the motor sector, construction grew more quickly than the economy as a whole. New construction totalled 2 billion marks in value in 1932. By 1934 it was 5.7 billion and by 1936, at 9 billion marks, it exceeded the peak year of the 1920s. The bulk of the construction was in residential housing (28 per cent) and road construction (21 per cent). The linkages established through construction with the rest of the economy were like those generated by motorisation. Demand increased rapidly for building materials and heavy machinery, for light tools and, in the case of motor vehicles, for more specialised industrial raw materials. The employment effects were also important. In 1933 only 666,000 were employed in the construction industries; by 1936 the figure was 2 million. It has been calculated that over 1.1 million jobs were more or less dependent on the motor vehicle and roads by 1938 [81: *82–3*]. The stimulus provided to these particular sectors also had the advantage of prompting further investment and expansion in the private economy and rapidly generating demand for ancillary goods and services. Small businesses were helped by the increase in private house-building and road construction, and private investment expanded more rapidly in both these sectors than private investment as a whole.

When government expenditure and investment is broken down in detail it becomes clear that no one sector on its own was capable of generating the growth necessary to explain the recovery (see Table XIII). If anything construction and motorisation have better claims than work-creation or rearmament. What was important was the aggregate effect of all the government's spending and

Table XIII *Public expenditure in Germany by category 1928–38 (bn RM)* *

	1928	1932	1933	1934	1935	1936	1937	1938
Total expenditure (central and local)	23.2	17.1	18.4	21.6	21.9	23.6	26.9	37.1
Construction	2.7	0.9	1.7	3.5	4.9	5.4	6.1	7.9
Rearmament	0.7	0.7	1.8	3.0	5.4	10.2	10.9	17.2
Transportation+	2.6	0.8	1.3	1.8	2.1	2.4	2.7	3.8
Work creation	–	0.2	1.5	2.5	0.8	–	–	–

* There is some overlap between the categories. Work-creation included some expenditure on roads; construction also includes some rearmament expenditure.
+ Figures for national expenditure on roads and waterways. Local expenditure averaged 0.6–0.8 bn RM from 1933–5.
Source: [3: *245*; 81: *81–2*; 86: *197*].

demand policies taken together, attacking the recession on a broad front, rather than at one particular point. Indeed the depression in Germany had been so severe and business confidence so reduced, that the government had no choice but to undertake a large part of the activity that private initiative was unwilling to undertake. This required the government, as Erbe has argued, to control and monitor the secondary effects of spending policies as well [28: *161–2*; 93: *972–4*]. The government did not simply pump money into the economy and wait for income to be generated by others. They used the spending policies as a lever to gain greater control over other areas of the economy. In the long run this helped to divert the economy to war purposes when the time came, and it also fitted in with the Nazis' own desire to control from above, to reduce the autonomy of the market and to produce an economy sensitive to the needs of the 'people'.

Thus government spending policies, although central to the explanation of the recovery, made necessary the extension of controls over the whole economy in order to make the system work. This was recognised by economic experts like Schacht as well as by the Nazis. Under the unusual political and economic circumstances of the early 1930s, the Nazis and their economic managers argued for a 'package' of policies that would allow them to regulate economic growth as a whole. The system could only be made to work with the addition of other controls, although they never quite amounted to a central economic plan. The most important of these additional controls were over prices and wages and over foreign trade. These were areas that had an important influence on the currency, and Schacht, among others, was as anxious to defend the currency and avoid inflation during the post-depression years as he had been during the 1920s. The controls over prices and wages helped to give the government's monetary policy a veneer of conservatism during the recovery period to compensate for unorthodox methods of financing. The controls over wages had another purpose as well. Wages were kept low, well below the real level of 1929–31, in the first years of recovery to give incentive to businessmen to expand business again with reduced labour costs. Unit labour costs, as Phelps-Brown has shown, did not reach the 1929–31 level throughout the 1930s [85: *438*].

The controls over foreign trade and foreign exchange, which had begun in 1931, were extended by the legislation arising out of Schacht's New Plan published in 1934. Here the purpose was to prevent government spending from being used to suck in imports for which the country could ill afford to pay. The collapse of world trade made it difficult to export goods, as did the deliberate over-valuation of the mark. In the face of overwhelming protectionism abroad and the closing of some traditional export markets in the United States and western Europe, it could be argued that Germany had little choice. In fact the control over trade matched the autarkic views of the agrarian and business supporters of the Nazi regime. Imports were to be substituted by domestic produc-tion, and the only trade allowed was in essential raw materials and foodstuffs that could not be produced at home. Much of this trade was carried on through bilateral barter agreements through which special clearing arrangements could be made to avoid pressure on the balance of payments and Germany's very small stock of gold and foreign exchange. Germany had such agreements with twenty-five countries by 1938 [77: *391–2*]. Such a policy effectively insulated the German economy against the impact of the world economy and avoided the international political and economic problems of the Weimar and depression period. But it also limited the growth of trade on which higher German economic growth depended.

Finally the government came to extend control over most of the remaining areas of the economy. These were predominantly of a supervisory rather than executive nature. Industry and trade were compelled to establish a network of territorial and industry-wide groups and chambers, although big business in particular needed little encouragement to complete a process of widespread cartelisation that had begun before the First World War and which was now designed to protect industrial interests in a period of economic and political uncertainty. Agriculture was also organised under the Reich Food Estate. Small businesses were supervised by the Chamber of Handicrafts. Banking, while fully restored to private ownership, became effectively an instrument of government policy. The capital market could only carry out those functions permitted by the state and all transactions were subject to approval. In this way the Nazi leadership was able to build up a structure of supervision that could be used at a later date for converting the economy more fully to war purposes, while it allowed those in charge of the recovery policies in the 1933–6 period to make sure that none of the variables at work in the German economy would undermine the effectiveness of the overall strategy.

Was this strategy Keynesian? Superficially, perhaps. But it is important to remember the differences. Keynes believed that expansionary policies required a low rate of interest: Schacht kept interest rates high throughout the early recovery period. Keynes argued that the marginal propensity to consume should be encouraged, and saving discouraged. In Germany the reverse happened. The same holds good for a prices and a wages policy, neither of which Keynes regarded as important under conditions of less than full employment. Keynes expected state expenditure to be used to push private enterprise along the road to recovery, and that private initiative would then take over. In Germany the state chose to control and regulate the secondary effects of spending policies as well in order to turn the economy in the direction favoured by the government. Finally Keynes hoped that such expansionary policies would be linked to a renewed expansion into the world economy and a large increase in private consumption. Neither occurred under Nazism [28: *169–77*; 55: *9–24*]. If a high level of state expenditure and of government control over the economy is a sufficient definition of Keynesianism then both Hitler and Stalin can be counted among its first practitioners. The evidence suggests, however, that in terms of both the letter and the spirit of the theory the German economic recovery was not Keynesian. It was instead the product of a wide range of increasingly coercive economic policies centred around government strategy to revive investment, control consumer demand and prepare for war.

5
State, industry and labour

Against the background of government recovery policies, the German economy continued to modernise itself under the impact of 'technological momentum'. That is, firms continued to innovate; to adopt new production methods; to devise new products; to break down the older ways of business and replace them with modern ones. The most noticeable shifts over the recovery period occurred in the continuing process of amalgamation and the elimination of the smaller marginal producers. This was nothing peculiar to the Nazi period. Levy had charted its progress through the 1920s in his book on *Industrial Germany* published in 1935 [62]. During the 1930s some 300,000 small businesses disappeared, while cartelisation became compulsory in those areas not already cartelised. High growth occurred in the new areas of the economy, in the motor industry, in chemicals, in the aircraft industry, in electrification. The more traditional goods, including foodstuffs and textiles, recovered only slowly and continued to decline as a proportion of German industrial output as they did in the other major industrial economies (see Table XIV). The pattern of investment reflected this. The heavy industrial sector expanded almost 200 per cent over the period 1932 to 1938; the consumer industries by only 38 per cent. Industrial investment was provided by the state and by funds produced within the firms themselves on the basis of expanding profits and a fall in costs, particularly of building, labour and raw materials.

To some extent the Nazi recovery owed its success to the normal development of technical and organisational change. Indeed it is tempting to see German growth during the 1930s, as Landes has done, as the product of an increased level of technological change

Table XIV *Index of production for selected German industries 1928–38*
(1928 = 100)

	1932	1933	1935	1938
Coal	69.4	72.7	94.8	123.0
Pig iron	33.3	44.5	108.8	154.3
Steel	39.3	52.2	112.6	162.2
Motor-cars	28.6	59.7	136.1	200.7
Commercial vehicles	22.9	40.7	121.7	200.7
Electrical energy	76.5	83.7	116.3	175.9
Machinery (on order)	32.8	39.1	111.8	166.7
Chemicals	50.9	58.5	79.5	127.0
Shoes	85.3	101.5	101.7	118.5
Textiles	79.2	90.5	91.0	107.5
Household goods, furniture	69.6	70.5	80.4	113.6

Source: [64: *46*], *Statistisches Jahrbuch für das Deutsche Reich 1938* (Berlin, 1939).

based around industries important for rearmament [61: *419–51*].
Yet for all these signs of change, the structural shifts were not as
great during the period as they had been before 1929 or after 1945.
Although there were technical and organisational changes they
were not sustained enough either to cause major structural shifts in
the economy or to explain the revival after 1932. If the productivity
growth of the period is put into perspective it becomes clear that
technical change or changes in organisation and work methods did
not play as important a part in helping recovery as they did during
the 1920s and 1950s. According to Rostas productivity grew only
1.3 per cent per annum during the 1929–38 period, despite the
fact that the high unemployment levels of the years 1930–4 gave an
involuntary boost to crude productivity figures [89]. Over the
period 1929 to 1936 productivity in Britain rose by 2.5 per cent
per annum. During the 1950s productivity in Germany grew at the
rate of 4.7 per cent each year.

Given the high priority accorded to investment by the government it is surprising that the productive performance of the
economy was not higher. In fact the absence of a high enough level
of technological and organisational change may well explain the
relatively modest multiplier impact in the 1930s already noted, and
the comparatively inefficient performance of the German war
economy that so surprised the British and American intelligence

officers when they surveyed German industry at the end of the war. There are a number of explanations. Much of the improvement in German industry was made in the 1920s in the 'rationalisation drive'. From 1929 onwards many large firms had considerable over-capacity and cut back heavily on investment. After 1932 there was little incentive to take up the task of modernisation again and the recovery was undertaken in many cases with plant and equipment installed before the depression. Firms were reluctant to have their fingers burned twice by investing heavily in a boom that might well peter out as had that of 1927–9. There was at the same time an insufficient demand pull to encourage firms, particularly in the newer industries, fully to adopt modern factory methods. Although the car industry expanded its productive performance rapidly, output per head in American car factories was still four times as great. The radio industry was similarly well behind that of America and Britain. The pattern of the recovery itself affected the productive performance of the economy. Many of the projects were labour-intensive, and the construction industry, which grew faster than many others, was particularly so.

Nor did governmental policies help to raise the level of efficiency. Firms were given government subsidies to take on additional workers. Many government contracts went to firms producing expensive and advanced equipment, such as aircraft, which were not particularly efficient users of either labour or capital. This fact reflected a more general problem. Because the state assumed increasing responsibility for the economy, and for large areas of investment in particular, the normal market pressures for improving efficiency and for innovating were often lacking. Instead it became necessary for the state itself to encourage a higher level of administrative and technical efficiency and this it seems to have been either unwilling or unable to achieve [16; 95]. Part of the explanation for this lies in the lack of detailed central planning. There was a plethora of controls but little predictive planning of output, or planning designed specifically to improve productive performance. Many firms complained of the stifling effect of government controls and bureaucracy and the lack of any clear division of responsibility. This growing bureaucratisation of the economy was not compensated for by any real effort to control what actually happened on the factory floor, despite the propaganda campaigns for more rationalisation. Instead the state provided contracts on a fixed cost-plus basis, encouraging firms to produce a high-priced end product at the expense of the taxpayer. High profits could be made out of safe government orders. It became less necessary for German firms to be competitive and productivity suffered accordingly.

Much of what industry did in the 1930s was determined not so much by economic considerations as by political circumstances. Mason has convincingly argued that the Third Reich saw the 'primacy of politics' in the economy [69]. Entrepreneurs were no longer in a position to make judgements that were independent of the political framework within which they were compelled to operate. To many historians this has seemed quite natural. The Nazi regime was put into power by big business to oppress labour and raise profits. Turner has questioned the first of these assumptions. Some big businessmen did contribute to the Nazi election funds but German capitalism cannot be regarded, on the evidence, as having collectively brought fascism to power in any direct sense [109]. Fascism in Germany was a mass movement brought to power through collusion with a bankrupt but traditional élite, not as the puppet of big business. If German capitalism bears any responsibility for the victory of Nazism it lies, as Nolte and Weisbrod have argued, in the failure of capitalism, and heavy industry in particular, to make the democratic regime work better, rather than in any positive desire to be governed by Nazis [80; 111].

It is of course true that there were areas where the interests of Nazism and big business appeared to coincide. Profits did rise under the Third Reich, though they were closely controlled. Not enough is yet known about profitability and industrial policy to say more [87]. Labour was oppressed and wages controlled. Schacht and other bankers and businessmen were given responsibility for the first three years of recovery and Hitler allowed them a considerable degree of autonomy in economic affairs. The Nazis accepted this because they needed recovery. But against this has to be set the fact that confidence in the private economy did not revive as it had done in the 1920s. Many businessmen were wary of long-term plans in case the boom petered out or the Nazis embarked on adventurism at home or abroad. There also existed very different interests among the various groups that made up German industry. These interests had become explicit in the arguments over policy during the depression. The divisions were still there during the Third Reich. Export-orientated firms demanded a higher level of trade throughout the 1930s but failed to get it. The manufacturers of consumer goods were at a permanent disadvantage in terms of investment and sales throughout the 1930s. For them low wages and government restrictions were the opposite of their economic interests. Even heavy industry, that had favoured some degree of autarky and state aid in the early 1930s, found that the extent of state control exercised after 1936, and the rise of a state-owned industrial sector, threatened their interests too. The strains that such a relationship produced have already been demonstrated for the car industry, the aircraft industry and the iron and steel industry; but much more research is needed to arrive at a satisfactory historical judgement of the relationship between Nazism and German business. What is already clear is that the Third Reich was not simply a businessman's regime underpinning an authoritarian capitalism but, on the contrary, that it set about reducing the autonomy of the economic élite and subordinating it to the interests of the Nazi state.

How far the political authority of the regime dictated the development of German business remains a more open question. There is little argument that the state adopted a more coercive and interventionist position during the period of accelerated war preparation from 1936. After that date the conservative influence over economic policy exercised by those such as Schacht declined. Göring, as head of the Four Year Plan organisation, brought the influence of the Party to bear more on the economic sphere. In November 1937 Schacht resigned as Minister of Economics and was replaced by a party hack, Walter Funk. Göring became, *de facto*, a kind of economic dictator [98]. As the state extended its role in supervising or regulating all the main economic variables, so there developed a more coherent economic system. German economists christened the system '*die gelenkte Wirtschaft*', the managed economy. Under such a system businessmen were regarded as economic functionaries serving the interests of the nation rather than as independent and enterprising creators of wealth. The concept of the 'managed economy' suited the regime's ideological ambitions, but stifled enterprise.

The relationship was not, however, all one-way. Some businesses found ways of adapting to the new conditions and flourished under them. Hayes has demonstrated that after an initial period of cautious co-operation, the chemical giant I. G. Farben was drawn more closely to the regime's ambitions because that was where its economic interests lay. I. G. Farben personnel joined the new Four Year Plan organisation, moving easily between the responsibilities of business and of state [45]. Businesses sought where they could to find patrons in the controlling apparatus who might protect or further their interests. There was no common business front, but there was room under the 'managed economy' for firms to shape their development not in terms of the pressures of the market (which for many firms were much reduced) but in bending, avoiding or defying the rules imposed upon them.

Here the cartel organisation, imposed compulsorily by the regime in 1934, proved useful to industry. Firms adopted defensive tactics from behind the shelter of the cartel walls. They fell back on their technical expertise to argue against particular policies, and used the solidarity of the cartel to obstruct or deflect unpopular directives. It also proved possible to use government subsidies, loopholes in the tax laws and loosely worded contracts to accumulate hidden reserves or additional productive capacity to strengthen the firm against its competitors [64: *126*]. There were, nonetheless, limits to what creative accounting or political manipulation could achieve. On important issues business had little influence; on issues that concerned the narrower interests of individual firms there was some room for manoeuvre.

Much the same could be said of the position of labour in the Third Reich. After 1933 government policy was directed to keeping wage rates low and removing all independent labour organisations which in the Weimar period had conducted collective bargaining over wages and conditions. Trade unions were closed down on 1 May 1933, and many union leaders imprisoned. The unions were replaced by a corporate institution, the Labour Front, which was made up of all employees and employers. In each factory Trustees of Labour were appointed by the Labour Front to act as agents between the authorities and the workforce. The

Trustees imposed a wage freeze. Strike action was outlawed and penalties for any form of industrial protest were severe. Recalcitrant workers were subjected to 'work-education weekends' by the Gestapo, or longer spells of confinement in a concentration camp. For the compliant workforce the Labour Front set up the Strength through Joy (*Kraft durch Freude*) organisation which provided lunch-time concerts and workers' holidays. The Beauty of Work movement was set up to make the factory a prettier place to work. Neither was a substitute for free wage-bargaining [68; 90].

It has long been assumed that labour, though it did not collectively resist the regime, was hostile to the dictatorship and never integrated with the new system. These views have been the subject of much recent criticism. The German working-class was not a homogeneous group but was divided, both before and after 1933, by occupation, region, sex and political outlook. The craft-workers of Bavaria were very different from the unionised metal-workers of Berlin. The attitude of labour to the Nazi regime can only be understood by a process of differentiation. Some elements of the working-class, particularly in small workshops or among non-unionised labour, supported the Nazi movement before 1933. It has been estimated that about one-fifth of Nazi voters and members were drawn from the manual work-force. After 1933 the numbers of workers in the Nazi Party went up, a product of opportunism perhaps as much as conviction.

If the working-class was not monolithic, neither was its experience of the new regime. There was room for improvement within the structure imposed by the Labour Front. Siegel has shown that while some employers were able to push wage rates below the agreed minima, others negotiated small increases with the Trustees in order to keep a skilled workforce together, or to fulfil essential state contracts [96: 35–6]. Wage-bargaining became unofficially sanctioned as long as it was confined to individual firms, or small groups of workers. This 'segmentation' of the workforce encouraged workers to compete against each other, and to pursue individual rather than collective interests. Bonuses and social payments (in the form of subsidised housing, or welfare provision) raised incomes above the wage norms, but also encouraged the compliance of the workforce. Hachtmann has shown that the fragmentation of labour matched the changing processes on the factory floor. With rationalised, large-scale production, employers and Labour Trustees co-operated to produce a sliding scale of wage rates to reward skill and effort, replacing the crude division into skilled, semi-skilled and unskilled that had dominated wage formation until then. The effect was not only to improve the overall skill level of the workforce by encouraging workers to train for higher wage grades, but to accentuate the 'segmentation' by offering the individual worker the opportunity for improvement at the expense of his or her fellows [43].

Labour also found its own ways to protect interests under the Labour Front. Research on the election to the Trustee councils suggests that, in the absence of the unions, workers saw the Trustees as a way of making their voice heard and participated with more enthusiasm than might have been expected. Some Trustees came from a social-democrat background; some had been workers' representatives on the works' councils set up in the 1920s. The Labour Front, because of its close links with the Nazi Party, could be manipulated by workers to force employers to make concessions. Workers, it seems, adopted the same strategies of adaptation and opportunism displayed by their employers. Veiled strikes, demarcation disputes, arguments over piece-rates, or absenteeism were some of the ways labour defended its interests [68]. Collective action was impossible. At the level of the individual firm, about which a great deal has still to be learned, the experience of labour varied greatly from one to another, and between one group and another in the same firm.

The net effect of these activities may well have prevented overall living-standards from falling further than they did. The government was committed to a general policy of wage restraint in the early years to encourage re-employment; from 1936 wage controls were designed to shift resources away from consumption towards heavy industry and war preparation. According to Nathan's calculations, the consumption of a range of important foodstuffs by German working-class families declined between 1927 and 1937, and those items where there was an increase tended to be the poorer, cheaper substitutes, such as potatoes and rye bread (see Table XV). Salary earners did better, though not much better when account is taken of higher tax payments and compulsory levies.

Table XV *Consumption in working-class families 1927 and 1937 (annual)* *

	1927	1937	% change
Rye bread (kg)	262.9	316.1	+ 20.2
Wheat bread (kg)	55.2	30.8	− 44.2
Meat and meat products (kg)	133.7	109.2	− 18.3
Bacon (kg)	9.5	8.5	− 10.5
Milk (ltr)	427.8	367.2	− 14.2
Cheese (kg)	13.0	14.5	+ 11.5
Eggs (number)	404	237	− 41.3
Fish (kg)	21.8	20.4	− 6.4
Vegetables (kg)	117.2	109.6	− 6.5
Potatoes (kg)	499.5	519.8	+ 4.1
Sugar (kg)	47.2	45.0	− 4.7
Tropical fruit (kg)	9.7	6.1	− 37.1
Beer (ltr)	76.5	31.6	− 58.7

* Adjusted for changes in purchasing-power and family size. Includes family budgets of low-paid civil servants and salaried workers.
Source: [76: *358*].

The effect of labour policies on economic performance is hard to assess quantitatively. The overall structure of the labour force changed relatively little during the 1930s. Labour input rose only slowly in the inter-war period compared with pre-1914 and post-1950. There was a slight movement from the countryside to the towns, which the regime tried to reverse. Services and government employment expanded, largely to fill new Party posts or to staff the offices of economic management and state regulation. Much labour was absorbed into low-paid work-creation, into the Labour Service or into the armed forces. These were areas of low or negligible income with small effects on the growth of the productive economy. With the coming of full employment more women were absorbed into the workforce, reaching a level of 37 per cent by 1939. Women were paid on average at little more than half the rate of men, and the ratio of skilled workers was much lower among the female workforce. Full employment exposed the rigidities of the existing labour market produced by wage restraint and the labour-intensive projects promoted by the regime. Long has calculated that both before and during the war the German economy made less efficient use of its labour resources than Britain or the United States [63: *16–18*]. Just as the regimentation of business restricted enterprise, so too did the system of low pay and limited mobility reduce the productive performance of the labour force. The 'economic miracle' of the 1950s and 1960s was characterised by large increases in labour input, high labour mobility and a steady appreciation of real incomes.

6
Full employment and the coming of war

In discussing economic recovery the historian should ask not only *why* it happened, but also what was the recovery *for?* In most cases the answer is economic – higher profits, sustained economic growth, higher living standards. In the case of the German recovery in the 1930s the answer was German imperialism and war. Historians disagree about what kind of war it was supposed to be, or the extent to which the economy was actually prepared for war, but there is no disagreement that the German economy was being prepared for some degree of military expansion.

What primarily concerns us here is not the course of diplomacy or German strategy but the effect of war preparation on economic growth. To understand this impact it is necessary to divide the period into two parts. From 1932 to 1936 the priority of the government was to achieve recovery through a combination of demand and investment policies. Rearmament was only a small part of the strategy. From 1936 to 1939, that is during the period of full employment, the priority switched to war preparation. The change in economic strategy was signalled by the second Four Year Plan set up in October 1936, which gave Göring responsibility for reorientating the economy for war and achieving self-sufficiency in essential war materials – oil, rubber and steel. During the second period it became necessary for the government to achieve control over all investment and trade to ensure that the economy moved in the directions necessary for war. It was also necessary to restrict the growth of private consumption in favour of state expenditure for military and economic preparations. 'The economy', Göring declared, 'must be completely converted for war.' In 1937–8 military expenditure increased to 10 billion marks, in 1938–9 to 17 billion, or 17 per cent of GNP. In addition much of the public investment that was not directly military was used for synthetic or substitute production whose purpose was to increase Germany's ability to wage war. When compared with any other major industrial power the proportion of the German economy geared to war was very significant.

It was during the period of growing war preparation that the limits of the German economic recovery were shown. It has already been pointed out that by any long-term measurement the achievement of the 1930s was not very remarkable. Even by 1937 the economy was only just above the level reached some twenty-five years before. From 1936 onwards all the indices of growth began to slow down. If the short-term recovery had been achieved with remarkable speed, the longer-term prospects for growth were much more muted. The switch to war preparation did not produce any real crisis in the economy before September 1939, but it did increasingly compromise the achievements already made.

One problem was finance. During 1938 the money supply grew much faster than output, 22 per cent against only 4 per cent growth in industrial output. The government's desire to increase war expenditure led to a continued expansion of the Reich debt and a growing diversion of resources away from the consumer sector. The competition for resources under conditions of full employment, rising world prices and raw material scarcity led to a veiled inflation that was only repressed by the government's strict enforcement of wage and price controls. The inflation itself might well have acted as a mild stimulus to growth had it not been for the fact that it stemmed from non-productive military expenditure and not from a rapid rise in consumer spending. Nor would it have mattered so much if output per man-hour had been expanding buoyantly, but that, too, was not the case.

Another problem was demand. After 1936 the government was anxious to cut the unrestricted growth of consumer demand in favour of war preparations. The slowing down of the growth of consumption affected overall economic growth and hence the ability of the economy to support the high levels of arms spending. Industrialists wanted the opposite to happen – more home demand, particularly for durables, and an expansion of exports to encourage high growth and technical change in the consumer industries. The Nazis did not want this. Instead it has been shown that they deliberately increased the marginal propensity to save and discouraged the growth of consumption. It was this switch to relatively less productive military expenditures that slowed up economic growth after 1936–7. In fact it was at just the point where government spending policies might have been expected to stimulate a sharp upswing in private business activity along Keynesian lines that the government chose to control that activity and divert much of it to war. The government moved, in Schumpeter's words, from 'additive' to 'substitutive' spending; from adding new resources to using resources that would otherwise have been taken up by private industry in a different way [93: *Vol. ii, 974*].

Some of these problems would have mattered less if the war industries had themselves been efficient and military expenditure been disbursed to encourage growth. But for a number of reasons they were not. Carroll has argued that it was administrative inefficiency that made rearmament industrially inefficient. Other historians have emphasised the structural problems: confused planning, labour shortages, poor factory organisation, excessive military interference [19; 73; 81]. One problem was the amount of money spent on organising and administering the military establishment instead of spending more on weapons and the industrial investment to produce them efficiently. Another problem was the amount of sheer financial waste produced by military or bureaucratic authorities with insufficient experience of industrial and management questions. Below these groups were industrialists either demoralised by the direction that Nazi policy was taking or happy to produce inefficiently at the government's and taxpayers' expense. No doubt all these factors contributed to the relatively poor growth effect that rearmament and war preparation produced.

Did all this amount to a crisis of the system as Mason has claimed? a crisis severe enough to push Hitler into war as the only way out of the economic dead-end produced by rearmament? There was certainly no crisis in the sense of a sharp down-turn in the business cycle. Nor was there any evidence of an increase in social protest or political resistance. The strains created by labour shortages, high deficit spending and the inefficient management of state contracts were real enough, a product of the exceptional economic circumstances produced by the growth of the military economy. Re-militarisation was only possible on such a scale under an extreme form of *dirigisme*, and with the enforced acquisition of additional resources in central Europe – from Austria, Czechoslovakia and, in 1939, from Poland. There is scant evidence, however, that these strains were capable of throwing the whole 'managed economy' out of control in 1939, and no evidence at all that Hitler's policy of war against Poland was a product of desperation prompted by the critical state of the economy. The final war crisis was a product of diplomatic and political forces largely detached from economic calculation [70; 82].

It is, of course, possible to argue that the economy could have performed very much better if it had not been distorted by the ideological imperatives imposed from above. Most economists are agreed that it could have grown faster if trade and consumer demand had been allowed to develop their own momentum out of the initial state-encouraged recovery [22; 53; 85]. Recovery later in the 1950s can be explained by high trade growth, expanding demand for consumer goods at home, and a political context in which business and labour co-operated to produce a vigorous market-orientated capitalism capable of generating high profits, rising earnings and welfare. It is arguable whether this kind of revival was possible in the 1930s, Nazi regime or not. The world economy did not support high trade growth; international co-operation for recovery foundered on things other than German economic nationalism; consensus between business and labour on a strategy for economic growth, while not impossible in the 1930s, was improbable. It is just as plausible to argue that without the intervention of the state from 1932 onwards in steering the recovery growth may well have settled at a level below that actually achieved, a level more consistent with the performance of Germany's European neighbours.

7

Conclusion

The debate on the German inter-war economy has not yet been completed but enough work has been done to fill in the important answers. More research is needed on the relationship between industry and government in the 1930s, and on questions to do with profitability and productivity. But on many aspects of the period it is possible to reach more definite conclusions.

The problems of economic growth during the inter-war years were nowhere so acute as in Germany. The structural problems of the world economy in the 1920s were exaggerated in their effect upon Germany because of the results of the war and inflation. These problems had already led to a downturn of business activity before the world slump occurred. The subsequent depression was then intensified by the fall in foreign lending and by government deflationary policies which were pursued partly because the un-orthodox alternatives were unacceptable, but largely because of internal and external political constraints. It was the combination of such constraints and the structural problems of the economy that forced the business cycle downwards to the point where many Germans were prepared to accept more radical alternatives, both Communist and National Socialist.

The triumph of the Nazi alternative in 1933 led to the introduction of a wide range of government policies designed to augment and speed up the existing recovery. Particular emphasis was put on investment-led growth and on public expenditure and fiscal concessions designed to expand demand. Before 1936 the bulk of expenditure was on work-creation, motorisation and general construction. After 1936 rearmament became more important. Throughout the 1933–9 period the government continued to extend the range of controls and to substitute public for private activity in order to pursue the political aims of the regime.

Did these controls amount to a fascist economic system? If the controls are looked at in isolation it can be seen that some, with the exception of the stringent labour laws, have been used to a greater or lesser extent by liberal western economies since the war. Many of the Nazi policies had their roots in the Weimar period. The thing to emphasise is that the controls and policies cannot be viewed on their own. If the policy instruments that the Nazis used have become conventional instruments by twentieth-century standards, the objectives of policy have not. It is impossible to view Nazi policies for the economy in isolation. They form a unit inseparable in the end from the political and ideological purposes of the regime. It is the political ends – the repression of labour, the controls over business, the plans for war, the racial programme – that distinguish the Nazi regime from its liberal successors. The Nazi 'economic system' became simply a part of the Nazi 'political' system, closer in character to the economy of Stalin's Russia than to those of the capitalist west.

Nevertheless German capitalism survived the experience of Nazism. The process of economic modernisation, if it owed little directly to the Nazis, was not reversed during the 1930s. Hitler tempered ideology with pragmatism, controlling but not transforming the economy as in Russia. Moreover business and labour found ways of diverting the full impact of the regime and defending their own interests. There were limits to the extent that the Nazis could divert the recovered economy to war purposes. Indeed what efforts were made to create an economy for waging war had the effect of slowing down recovery and growth, stifling initiative and creating business uncertainty once again. 'Recovery' in this context was a dead end.

Bibliography

The following list is a guide to the existing English language literature on the recovery. The most important books in German have been included where there is no ready translation available.

[1] D. Abraham (1981) *The Collapse of the Weimar Republic* (Princeton, N.J.). Much-criticised account of the politics of the German business community and the rise of Hitler.

[2] D. Aldcroft (1978) *The European Economy 1914–70* (London).

[3] S. Andic, and J. Veverka (1964) 'The Growth of Government Expenditure in Germany since the Unification', *Finanzarchiv*, 23.

[4] H. Arndt (1944) *Economic Lessons of the Nineteen-Thirties* (London).

[5] F. Baerwald (1934) 'How Germany Reduced Unemployment', *American Economic Review*, 24. A useful discussion of the impact of recovery policies on different industries.

[6] T. Balderston (1977) 'The German Business Cycle in the 1920s: a Comment', *Economic History Review*, 2nd ser., 30.

[7] T. Balderston (1993) *The Origins and Course of the German Economic Crisis 1923–1932* (Berlin). Comprehensive survey of the causes of the slump. Highlights poor demand for exports and low investment as primary causes.

[8] T. Balogh (1938) 'The National Economy of Germany', *Economic Journal*, 48. A pioneering analysis of the Nazi economy, placing emphasis on re-militarisation to explain its growth and structure.

[9] A. Barkai (1990) *Nazi Economics: Ideology, Theory and Policy* (Oxford). Argues that ideology played an important part in shaping policy choices in the economy under Nazism.

[10] E. Bennett (1962) *Germany and the Diplomacy of the Financial Crisis, 1931* (New York).

[11] R. Bessell (1978) 'Eastern Germany as a Structural Problem in the Weimar Republic', *Social History*, 3.

[12] W. A. Boelcke (1983) *Die deutsche Wirtschaft 1930–1945* (Düsseldorf). Argues that Schacht pursued an orthodox, conservative

strategy until 1936 when Göring began to transform the economy along more ideological lines.

[13] K. Borchardt (1991) *Perspectives on Modern German Economic History and Policy* (Cambridge). Argues that the government had little room for manoeuvre at the height of the slump, given existing economic and political constraints.

[14] R. A. Brady (1943) *Business as a System of Power* (New York). A Marxist view, which sees the economy in the 1930s as the logical outcome of the strategies of German big business.

[15] H-J. Braun (1990) *The German Economy in the Twentieth Century* (London). The most up-to-date general account.

[16] C. Bresciani-Turroni (1938) 'The Multiplier in Practice', *Review of Economic Statistics*, 20.

[17] G. Bry (1960) *Wages in Germany 1871–1945* (Princeton, N.J.). A full statistical survey on German earnings.

[18] W. Carr (1972) *Arms, Autarky and Aggression* (London). Emphasises the importance of political and ideological influences on economic policy under Hitler.

[19] B. A. Carroll (1968) *Design for Total War: Arms and Economics in the Third Reich* (The Hague). A major study of the militarised economy in the 1930s. Emphasises the inefficiencies of the military-economic complex.

[20] F. Child (1958) *The Theory and Practice of Exchange Control in Germany* (London).

[21] W. Conze (ed.) (1967) *Die Staats- und Wirtschaftskrise des Deutschen Reiches*. Useful essays on the depression, particularly by Keese on problems of growth.

[22] G. Cormi (1990) *Hitler and the Peasants: Agrarian Policy in the Third Reich* (Oxford).

[23] J. S. Davis (1975) *The World between the Wars, 1919–1939: an Economist's View* (London). Blames the crisis in Germany on the withdrawal of short-term foreign loans.

[24] W. Deist (1981) *The 'Wehrmacht' and German Rearmament* (London). Detailed study of the military build-up. Stresses its slow and poorly co-ordinated development.

[25] B. Eichengreen (1992) *Golden Fetters: the Gold Standard and the Great Depression 1919–1939* (Oxford). Argues persuasively that the crisis was conditioned by the failure of the international currency and payments system.

[26] B. Eichengreen (1992) 'The Origins and Nature of the Great Slump Revisited', *Economic History Review*, 45.

[27] H. S. Ellis (1941) *Exchange Controls in Central Europe* (Cambridge, Mass.).

[28] R. Erbe (1958) *Die nationalsozialistische Wirtschaftspolitik 1933–9 im*

Lichte der modernen Theorie (Zürich). An important contribution to the debate on economic recovery. Emphasises rearmament as a key to growth, and shows that the economic strategy was far from Keynesian.

[29] W. Eucken (1948) 'On the Theory of the Centrally Administered Economy: an Analysis of the German Experiment', *Economica*, 15.

[30] M. E. Falkus (1975) 'The German Business Cycle in the 1920s', *Economic History Review*, 2nd ser., 28. Argues that foreign lending was the critical factor in the recession rather than a domestically induced downturn.

[31] J. E. Farquharson (1976) *The Plough and the Swastika: the NSDAP and Agriculture in Germany 1928–1945* (London).

[32] G. D. Feldman (1969) 'The Social and Economic Policies of German Big Business 1918–1929', *American Historical Review*, 75.

[33] W. Fischer and P. Czada (1970) 'Wandlungen in der deutschen Industriestruktur im 20 Jahrhundert', in G. Ritter (ed.), *Entstehung und Wandel der modernen Gesellschaft* (Berlin). An important long-term assessment of structural change in the German economy.

[34] H. Fleisig (1976) 'War-Related Debts and the Great Depression', *American Economic Review*, 66. Argues that reduction of US lending and curtailment of US imports caused the recession. Stresses work-creation in Nazi recovery policies.

[35] N. Forbes (1987) 'London Banks, the German Standstill Agreements and Economic Appeasement in the 1930s', *Economic History Review*, 2nd ser., 40. Shows how credit lines were kept open to Germany from London during the recovery period.

[36] J. A. Garraty (1973) 'The New Deal, National Socialism and the Great Depression', *American Historical Review*, 78. Not entirely convincing comparison of German recovery strategy and the American New Deal.

[37] G. Garvy (1975) 'Keynes and the Economic Activists of Pre-Hitler Germany', *Journal of Political Economy*, 83. Shows that Keynesian theory had been anticipated in German theoretical discussion before and during the depression.

[38] D. Gessner (1977) 'Agrarian Protectionism in the Weimar Republic', *Journal of Contemporary History*, 12. A useful analysis of a central component of 'interest-group' politics.

[39] J. Gillingham (1985) *Industry and Politics in the Third Reich* (London). A case study of the German coal industry under Nazism.

[40] W. Glastetter, G. Högemann and R. Marquardt (1991) *Die wirtschaftliche Entwicklung in der Bundesrepublik Deutschland 1950–1989* (Frankfurt am Main). An excellent survey of the long-run determinants of economic development in Germany in the twentieth century.

[41] L. Grebler (1937) 'Work-Creation Policy in Germany 1932–5', Parts I and II, *International Labour Review*, 35.

[42] C. Guillebaud (1939) *The Economic Recovery of Germany 1933–1938* (London). Unpopular at the time of publication, the book was the first serious attempt to analyse the performance of the German economy under Hitler. Puts rearmament into perspective and details the wide number of policy instruments used to achieve recovery.

[43] R. Hachtmann (1989) *Industriearbeit im 'Dritten Reich'* (Göttingen). An essential survey of the changing wage-structures and patterns of labour utilisation during the Nazi period.

[44] G. Hallgarten (1952) 'Adolf Hitler and German Heavy Industry 1931–33', *Journal of Economic History*, 12. Argues that big business played a critical part in Hitler's rise to power.

[45] P. Hayes (1987) *Industry and Ideology: I.G. Farben in the Nazi Era* (Cambridge). Argues that German industries adopted a flexible and adaptive attitude to the regime in line with their primary economic interests.

[46] P. Hayes (1993) 'Polycracy and Policy in the Third Reich: the Case of the Economy' in T. Childers and J. Caplan (eds.), *Re-evaluating the Third Reich* (London).

[47] J. L. Heinemann (1969) 'Count von Neurath and German Policy at the London Economic Conference, 1933', *Journal of Modern History*, 31.

[48] W. Hoffmann (1965) *Das Wachstum der deutschen Wirtschaft seit der Mitte des 19 Jahrhunderts* (Berlin). Essential statistical survey of German economic growth. Figures for the 1920s have been subject to considerable criticism.

[49] K. Holl (ed.) (1978) *Wirtschaftskrise und liberale Demokratie* (Göttingen). Contains a useful article by Feldman on industrial strategy during the depression.

[50] T. Hughes (1969) 'Technological Momentum in History: Hydrogenation in Germany 1898–1933', *Past & Present*, 15.

[51] H. James (1986) *The German Slump: Politics and Economics 1924–1936* (Oxford). Essential study of the political economy of Germany during recession. Argues that early recovery was brought about by a modest consumer boom, followed by high levels of rearmament and a more statist economic policy.

[52] H. James (1992) 'Innovation and Conservatism in Economic Recovery: the Alleged "Nazi Recovery" of the 1930s' in W. Garside (ed.), *Capitalism in Crisis: International Responses to the Great Depression* (London). Argues that the recovery policies were orthodox, even conservative, in character.

[53] D. E. Kaiser (1980) *Economic Diplomacy and the Origins of the Second World War: Germany, Britain, France and Eastern Europe 1930–1939* (Princeton, N.J.).

[54] I. Kershaw (ed.) (1990) *Weimar: Why Did German Democracy Fail?* (London). Useful essays on the policy options during the crisis.

[55] J. M. Keynes (1933) *The Means to Prosperity* (London).

[56] C. Kindleberger (1973) *The World in Depression 1929–1939* (London). Stresses the role of short-term lending in sharpening the crisis in Germany. Less valuable on the recovery period.

[57] B. H. Klein (1959) *Germany's Economic Preparations for War* (Cambridge, Mass.). Argues that rearmament was not important until at least 1936–7 and that its impact thereafter has been exaggerated.

[58] J. J. Klein (1956) 'German Money and Prices 1933–1944' in M. Friedman (ed.), *Studies in the Quantity Theory of Money* (Chicago).

[59] J. von Kruedener (ed.) (1990) *Economic Crisis and Political Collapse: the Weimar Republic* (Oxford). Essential reading on the arguments surrounding the Borchardt thesis.

[60] J. Kuczynski (1945) *Germany. Economic and Labour Conditions under Fascism* (London).

[61] D. Landes (1970) *The Unbound Prometheus* (Cambridge). Lays emphasis on the role of US lending in explaining the German slump. Less useful on the recovery, but a stimulating analysis of the late 1930s military economy.

[62] H. Levy (1935) *Industrial Germany* (Cambridge).

[63] C. D. Long (1958) *The Labor Force under Changing Income and Employment* (Princeton, N.J.).

[64] S. Lurie (1947) *Private Investment in a Controlled Economy: Germany 1933–1939* (London). An important guide to German investment policy and the structural changes in the capital market.

[65] A. Maddison (1964) *Economic Growth in the West* (London).

[66] A. Maddison (1972) 'Growth and Fluctuations in the World Economy 1870–1960', *Banca Nazionale del Lavoro Quarterly* (Sept.).

[67] K. Mandelbaum (1944) 'An Experiment in Full Employment: Controls in the Germany Economy 1933–8' in Oxford University Institute of Statistics, *The Economics of Full Employment* (Oxford). Argues that growth in the 1930s could have been higher.

[68] T. W. Mason (1966) 'Labour in the Third Reich, 1933–1939', *Past & Present*, 12.

[69] T. W. Mason (1968) 'The Primacy of Politics – Politics and Economics in National Socialist Germany' in S. Woolf (ed.), *The Nature of Fascism* (London). Seminal discussion of the relationship between German capitalism and the Nazi state.

[70] T. W. Mason (1992) *Social Policy in the Third Reich* (Oxford). Argues that the failure to integrate labour into the Nazi state produced growing social tension and economic crisis by the late 1930s which coloured Hitler's decision to launch war in 1939.

[71] R. Meister (1991) *Die grosse Depression: Zwangslagen und Handlungs-*

spielräme der Wirtschafts- und Finanzpolitik in Deutschland 1929–1932 (Regensburg). A detailed examination of the alternative policies advocated during the slump. Suggests that public works in 1931 would have permitted earlier recovery.

[72] S. Merlin (1943) 'Trends in German Economic Control since 1933', *Quarterly Journal of Economics*, 62.

[73] A. S. Milward (1965) *The German Economy at War* (London). Argues that military spending and armaments output were limited before 1941, until military reverses forced the regime to adopt total war.

[74] E. B. Mittelman (1938) 'The German Use of Unemployment Insurance Funds for Works Purposes', *Journal of Political Economy*, 46.

[75] H. Mommsen, D. Petzina and B. Weisbrod (eds.) (1973) *Industrielles System und politische Entwicklung in der Weimarer Republik* (Düsseldorf).

[76] O. Nathan and M. Fried (1944) *The Nazi Economic System* (Durham, N.C.).

[77] L. Neal (1979) 'The Economics and Finance of Bilateral Clearing Agreements: Germany 1934–8', *Economic History Review*, 2nd ser., 32.

[78] F. Neumann (1942) *Behemoth: the Structure and Practice of National Socialism* (London). An important theoretical discussion; argues that the Nazi economy was a 'command economy' run on behalf of state monopoly capitalism.

[79] A. J. Nicholls (1994) *Freedom with Responsibility: the Social Market Economy in Germany 1918–1963* (Oxford).

[80] E. Nolte (1969) 'Big Business and German Politics: a Comment', *American Historical Review*, 75.

[81] R. J. Overy (1987) 'Unemployment in the Third Reich', *Business History*, 29.

[82] R. J. Overy (1994) *War and Economy in the Third Reich* (Oxford). Essays on recovery, rearmament and war economy.

[83] M. Palyi (1941) 'Economic Foundations of the German Totalitarian State', *American Journal of Sociology*, 46. Discusses the anti-capitalist nature of the Nazi regime.

[84] D. Petzina (1969) 'Germany and the Great Depression', *Journal of Contemporary History*, 4. Stresses internal rather than external political pressures on Brüning, particularly from the agricultural lobby.

[85] E. H. Phelps-Brown (1968) *A Century of Pay* (London). Useful figures on the long-term development of the German economy.

[86] K. E. Poole (1939) *German Financial Policies 1932–1939* (Harvard). Stresses role played in the recovery by government spending. Critical of public works.

[87] A. von Riel and A. Schram (1993) 'Weimar Economic Decline,

Nazi Economic Recovery and the Stabilisation of Political Dictatorship', *Journal of Economic History*, 53.

[88] W. Röpke (1933) 'Trends in German Business Cycle Policy', *Economic Journal*, 43. Detail on the alternative policies proposed to solve unemployment from one of those closely involved in the discussions.

[89] L. Rostas (1943) 'Industrial Production, Productivity and Distribution in Britain, Germany and the United States', *Economic Journal*, 53.

[90] S. Salter (1983) 'Structures of Consensus and Coercion: Workers' Morale and the Maintenance of Work Discipline' in D. Welch (ed.), *Nazi Propaganda* (London).

[91] H. Schacht (1949) *Account Settled* (London). A rather insubstantial survey of German policy in the 1930s by Hitler's economics minister. Useful in demonstrating continuities across the 1933 divide.

[92] S. Schuker (1988) *American 'Reparations' to Germany* (Princeton, N.J.). Argues that Germany benefited from the flow of foreign investment, much of which was never repaid.

[93] J. Schumpeter (1939) *Business Cycles* (2 vols., New York). Suggests that government played a key role in the upswing, at the expense of private business and consumption. Sees the revival of agriculture and foreign trade and exchange controls as the key elements of the recovery package.

[94] A. Schweitzer (1964) *Big Business in the Third Reich* (Bloomington, Ind.). Major study of the Nazi economy, stressing the importance of rearmament for recovery.

[95] A. Schweitzer (1946) 'Profits under Nazi Planning', *Quarterly Journal of Economics*, 60.

[96] T. Siegel (1985) 'Wage Policy in the Third Reich', *Politics and Society*, 14. Essential summary of the latest research on wages under the Nazi regime, which demonstrates the weakened position of labour and the suppression of wage growth.

[97] A. E. Simpson (1969) *Hjalmar Schacht in Perspective* (The Hague).

[98] A. E. Simpson (1959) 'The Struggle for Control of the German Economy 1936–7', *Journal of Modern History*, 21. Argues convincingly that there occurred a clear break in Nazi economic policy in 1936–7, with an increase in state power.

[99] A. Sohn-Rethel (1978) *Economy and Class-Structure of German Fascism* (London). Account from a Marxist economist who worked in Germany in the slump. Useful analysis of the divisions in the German business community.

[100] G. Spencely (1979) 'R. J. Overy and the *Motorisierung*: a Comment', *Economic History Review*, 2nd ser., 32. Sees construction as the key recovery sector.

[101] P. Stachura (1988) *Unemployment in the Great Depression in Germany* (London).

[102] D. Stegemann, B. Wendt and P-C. Witt (eds.) (1978) *Industrielle Gesellschaft und politisches System* (Bonn). Contains a useful article by Jochmann critical of Brüning's deflation.

[103] G. Stolper (1967) *The German Economy: 1870 to the Present* (London). Gives considerable emphasis to agriculture in the slump and recovery. Attributes revival to public spending but argues that recovery might have gone further without the Nazis.

[104] I. Svennilson (1954) *Growth and Stagnation in the European Economy* (Geneva). An important analysis of the causes of the slump and revival in Europe. Attributes stagnation to slow growth of demand and fall in trade.

[105] M. Sweezy (1940) 'German Corporate Profits 1926–1938', *Quarterly Journal of Economics*, 54.

[106] P. Temin (1971) 'The Beginning of the Depression in Germany', *Economic History Review*, 2nd ser., 24. Argues that domestic factors were more important than foreign in causing the German slump.

[107] P. Temin (1990) 'Socialism and Wages in the Recovery from the Great Depression in the US and Germany', *Journal of Economic History*, 50. Argues that full employment in Germany was a result of low wage policy.

[108] J. Thies (1978) 'Hitler's European Building Programme', *Journal of Contemporary History*, 13.

[109] H. A. Turner (1985) *German Big Business and the Rise of Hitler* (Oxford). Argues that German business did not act collectively to support the Nazi Party. An indispensable survey of business attitudes to recession.

[110] H-E. Volkmann (1990) 'The National-Socialist Economy in Preparation for War' in W. Deist et al., *Germany and the Second World War: Vol. I* (Oxford). Argues that the economy from 1933 was geared, indirectly and directly, to war preparation within an anti-liberal, autarkist structure.

[111] B. Weisbrod (1979) 'Economic Power and Political Stability Reconsidered: Heavy Industry in Weimar Germany', *Social History*, 4.

[112] T. de Witt (1978) 'The Economics and Politics of Welfare in the Third Reich', *Central European History*, 11.

[113] M. Wolfe (1955) 'The Development of Nazi Monetary Policy', *Journal of Economic History*, 15.

[114] S. Woolf (1968) 'Did a Fascist Economic System Exist?' in Woolf (ed.), *The Nature of Fascism* (London). Stresses importance of the investment boom of the 1930s and the spread of an interdependent network of controls.

[115] W. S. Woytinsky (1961) *Stormy Passage* (London).

Index

New Studies in Economic and Social History

Titles in the series available from Cambridge University Press:

Previously published as

Studies in Economic History

Titles in the series available from the Macmillan Press Limited

Economic History Society

The Economic History Society, which numbers around 3,000 members, publishes the *Economic History Review* four times a year (free to members) and holds an annual conference.

Enquiries about membership should be addressed to

The Assistant Secretary
Economic History Society
PO Box 70
Kingswood
Bristol
BS15 5TB

Full-time students may join at special rates.